D1617390

CHRIST OUR JOY

MSGR. JOSEPH MURPHY

CHRIST OUR JOY

THE THEOLOGICAL VISION
OF
POPE BENEDICT XVI

IGNATIUS PRESS   SAN FRANCISCO

Front cover photograph of Pope Benedict XVI
by Stefano Spaziani, Rome

Cover design by Roxanne Mei Lum

© 2008 Ignatius Press, San Francisco
All rights reserved
ISBN 978-1-58617-182-7
Library of Congress Control Number 2006939358
Printed in the United States of America ∞

To His Eminence Angelo Cardinal Sodano

Dean of the College of Cardinals

Secretary of State
to Pope John Paul II and to Pope Benedict XVI
(1991–2006)

grato ex animo

CONTENTS

Preface		ix
Acknowledgments		xv
Acknowledgments to Copyright Holders		xvii
Abbreviations		xix
Introduction		1
I.	A World in Need of Joy	19
	1. Boredom	24
	2. Acedia	31
	3. Meaninglessness	36
	4. The Gospel of Joy	39
II.	Joy and Truth	44
III.	Living Joy in Faith, Hope, and Love	62
	1. Faith	62
	2. Hope	66
	3. Love	68
IV.	The Trinity	77
	1. The name of God	78
	2. The Trinity of love	86
V.	Creation	99
VI.	Jesus Christ, Bearer of Joy	113
	1. Approaches to the mystery of Jesus Christ	115

2. The prayer of Jesus   120
3. The death and resurrection of Jesus   131

VII. The Spirit of Eternal Joy   139
1. The Son and the Spirit   141
2. The Spirit and the Church   148
3. The Holy Spirit and Christian existence   152

VIII. The Church, Guardian of Joy   159

IX. Eucharistic Joy   171

X. Joy, Suffering, and Death   184

XI. Eternal Joy   195

Conclusion   203
Bibliography   207

PREFACE

From the first moment of his appearance on the balcony of St. Peter's Basilica as the newly elected successor of St. Peter on April 19, 2005, Pope Benedict XVI has exuded joy. Not only that: joy has been one of the main themes in his formal and informal addresses as Pope. This joy took many by surprise, since the worldwide image of Cardinal Joseph Ratzinger up to then was that of the *Panzerkardinal*, the Grand Inquisitor, a kill-joy. It was he, after all, who silenced liberal theologians and spoke uncomfortable truths (mostly "out of season"), those perennial truths that define the Church's message and mission but which were either being denied or ignored by faithful and skeptic alike. And, even today, many wonder about the change. Was it simply a change of perspective on our part or did he himself undergo a change on election to the See of Peter? Both questions can be answered, at least in part, in the affirmative.

Before his election, the world at large (and this includes most theologians, clerics, and engaged laity, who are often more influenced by the secular media than they care to admit) knew Joseph Ratzinger simply as the Cardinal Prefect of the Congregation for the Doctrine of the Faith, an office he held for over twenty-three years. The Congregation has the task of ensuring that the faith handed on by the apostles and their successors is preserved intact and handed on faithfully to the next generations. The controversial decisions of this Congregation—published under his signature and generally presented to the world's press by the Cardinal

Prefect in person—made headlines across the globe. These decisions were usually in conflict with the prevailing values embraced by the Western media in particular, not infrequently rousing their hostility. The result was an attack on Ratzinger himself, as though he were personally responsible for the decisions, rather than the Congregation over which he presided.

Few were aware that the former professor of dogma and the history of dogma at the University of Regensburg (a title he still proudly claims) continued to publish as a private theologian and to enter into the scholarly debate even as Cardinal Prefect. Many of his more recent articles and books, it seems to me, were either part of his own "homework" during the preparation of various documents produced by the Congregation or by one of the two commissions he chaired as Cardinal Prefect (the International Theological Commission and the Pontifical Biblical Commission) or written in the wake of some particularly controversial document, such as *Dominus Iesus*, to defend its message. In any case, his own theology is much richer than the bare bones of the Church's teaching found in those official documents (for example, *Truth and Tolerance*, the collection of papers that contain his own original and subtle theology of the relationship between faith and the world's religions, takes up and develops in a creative way the teaching of *Dominus Iesus*). These "private" writings were, on the one hand, rooted in his earlier academic research and publications and can be understood only in the light of those writings. On the other hand, his "private" publications develop (and correct) many of the ideas first adumbrated in his original research. The sad fact is that these theological writings were rarely read by mainline theologians of the post-Vatican II establishment—indeed many theologians in the English-speaking world did not even know of their existence. Now at last (not least thanks to his election as Pope) they are being discovered as fresh sources of inspiration by a new generation of theologians.

It must be admitted that the very office he held as Cardinal Prefect lent itself to the negative image of the media. His task was not unlike that of a customs officer—to decide what could be admitted and what had to be kept out. This unwelcome task, which, I am personally convinced, ran against the grain of his own personality, was exacerbated by the situation of the Church at the time—the aftermath of a major council. Most councils of necessity disturb the Church for generations, until such time as the dust finally settles. The Second Vatican Council created perhaps more of an upheaval than most other councils, since in its aftermath there was a radical overhaul of the Church's rituals, her self-understanding, and her mission. The pontificates of both Pope Paul VI and John Paul II were mainly devoted to translating the decisions of the Council into daily practice—and, under John Paul II, Cardinal Ratzinger as Prefect played a significant role in determining yet again the parameters of the Church's dogmatic and moral teaching essential for authentic Christian living and theological reflection. The Magisterium of both pontiffs found its expression in numerous liturgical texts, authoritative documents, codes of Canon Law, and the *Catechism of the Catholic Church*. With the death of John Paul II, that initial period of authentic interpretation of the Council came to an end.

With the election of Benedict XVI, not only has a new (and, hopefully, calmer) era dawned but, as it were, the customs officer is now at home, where he can take off his uniform and be himself with his family. This is a new perspective for the world at large. But for those of us who were privileged to study under him and to meet with him regularly for the past thirty-five years or so, what all now see in the media (and meet in private capacity) is the same person we knew of old, the same alert mind, kind heart, and impish eyes. His election as Pope, therefore, did bring about one important change. He can now speak on his own terms to the Church and to the world as pastor and theologian—for him both terms are almost interchangeable, since theology is about the ultimate truth of our existence that heals and sets us free, inner liberation being the end of all pastoral activity. As Cardinal Prefect, he had to set limits; now he can expand to embrace the whole message, the whole Christ, and present him to the world. As Prefect, he had to say no. Now he can often say yes, and so he invites our materially rich but spiritually impoverished generation to taste and see that the Lord is good, to find joy once again.

Early on, Joseph Murphy noticed how central the term "joy" was in the addresses of Pope Benedict XVI. This led him on a voyage of discovery through the many writings of the former Joseph Ratzinger, only to find that the theme of joy has in various degrees pervaded all his theology. Joy is not a new topic for Joseph Ratzinger, but has been one of his major concerns as a theologian and pastor. But Murphy has gone further than that. He recognizes the Pope's invitation to joy as a key to understanding Ratzinger's basic theological vision. Monographs and dissertations have been written (especially in German and Italian) on various aspects of his theology. More recently, we have been inundated with biographies and articles on his person and the role he played in the Church over the past half-century. Still rare are publications dealing with his theological vision in all its depth and originality. Joseph Murphy's beautifully written work is the exception. In this book, he takes up the often fragmentary but seminal ideas of Joseph Ratzinger, and he develops them in his own creative way, while placing them within the broader canvas of Ratzinger's theological writings. This book has one objective: to induce the reader to engage personally with the original and creative mind of Joseph Ratzinger—professor, pastor, and now Pope.

> D. Vincent Twomey, S.V.D.
> Maynooth
> Feast of the Exaltation of the Cross, 2006

ACKNOWLEDGMENTS

This book originated in a series of conversations on some central themes in the writings of Pope Benedict XVI held in October 2005 with the community of the *Dominicaines du Saint-Esprit* at their motherhouse in Pontcalec, France. Their interest in the Holy Father's theological and spiritual work prompted me to further my research into the theme of joy as a key to understanding Pope Benedict's thought. To Mother Marie-Geneviève Venard, O.P., then Prioress General, and to all the members of the institute go my heartfelt thanks.

I owe a special debt of gratitude to Fr. D. Vincent Twomey, S.V.D., member of the Ratzinger *Schülerkreis* and professor emeritus of moral theology at St. Patrick's College, Maynooth, who very kindly agreed to write the preface to this work. I am grateful to him for his encouragement, assistance, and advice at every stage in the composition of this book.

I also wish to thank all those who read and commented on earlier drafts: Fr. Patrick Burke; Msgr. Michael Crotty; Fr. Terence Crotty, O.P.; Fr. John M. Cunningham, O.P.; Fr. Martin Henry; Fr. Seamus Horgan; Fr. Eamonn McLaughlin; Fr. Thomas Norris; Msgr. James O'Brien; Fr. James O'Kane; and Mr. Oliver Ryan. Their suggestions and observations have contributed in no small way to the overall improvement of this work.

Finally, I thank Fr. Joseph Fessio, S.J. and Ignatius Press for having accepted the manuscript for publication. My gratitude goes in a particular way to the dedicated team at

Ignatius Press, including Nellie Boldrick, Carolyn Rae Lemon, and their freelancer Darlene Broussard, who carefully worked on the manuscript, patiently and promptly answered the author's frequent questions, and brought the book through the various stages of editing and production.

May God's abundant blessings be ever with them. *Beannacht Dé orthu go léir!*

ACKNOWLEDGMENTS
TO COPYRIGHT HOLDERS

I thank the following copyright holders who kindly granted permission to reproduce excerpts from various works:

— Catholic University of America Press for permission to quote from Joseph Ratzinger, *Eschatology: Death and Eternal Life.* © 1988, CUA Press, Washington, D.C.

— Crossroad Publishing Company for permission communicated through the Copyright Clearance Center to quote from Joseph Ratzinger/Pope Benedict XVI, *The Yes of Jesus Christ: Exercises in Faith, Hope and Love.* © 2005, Crossroad Publishing Company, New York.

— Ignatius Press for permission to quote from various works of Joseph Ratzinger, in English translation, for which it holds the copyright.

— International Catholic Journal *Communio* for permission to quote from Michael Hanby, "The Culture of Death, the Ontology of Boredom, and the Resistance of Joy", in *Communio* (American edition) 31 (2004): 181–99 and from Jean-Charles Nault, "Acedia: Enemy of Spiritual Joy", in *Communio* (American edition) 31 (2004): 236–59.

— Libreria Editrice Vaticana for permission to quote from the writings, homilies, and addresses of Pope Benedict XVI and from the *Catechism of the Catholic Church,*

ABBREVIATIONS

Apart from standard abbreviations for biblical books, the following are used:

CCSL   Corpus Christianorum Series Latina

DS   Heinrich Denzinger, Adolf Schönmetzer. *Enchiridion Symbolorum Definitionum et Declarationum de Rebus Fidei et Morum*, 36th ed. Freiburg in Breisgau: Herder, 1965.

OR   *L'Osservatore Romano*, weekly English-language edition

PG   Patrologia Graeca (Migne)

PL   Patrologia Latina (Migne)

INTRODUCTION

"Joy" is a word seldom far from the lips of the Holy Father, Pope Benedict XVI. Frequently repeated in his homilies and addresses, it has emerged as one of the key themes of his pontificate. The notion of joy is an attractive one, for it is something we all seek. By evoking joy and associating it intimately with the life of faith, Pope Benedict invites us to ponder on what it really means to be Christian and on the effects that the Christian faith should produce in our lives. Joy is characteristic of the Christian, for it flows from the very heart of what Christianity is about: the merciful love of God the Father, made known to us through the saving work of the Son and the indwelling of the Holy Spirit of love in the Church and in our souls.

Addressing his fellow Cardinals on the day before his election to the Chair of Peter, the then Cardinal Joseph Ratzinger spoke of the pastoral ministry, recalling Christ's command to the apostles to bear fruit that will last (see Jn 15:16). Explaining that the fruit in question is all that has been sown in human hearts—"love, knowledge, a gesture capable of touching hearts, words that open the soul to joy in the Lord"—he prayed that the Lord would "once again give us a Shepherd according to his own heart, a Shepherd who will guide us to knowledge of Christ, to his love and to true joy".[1]

---

[1] Cardinal Joseph Ratzinger, Homily at the Mass for the election of the Roman Pontiff, April 18, 2005, in the weekly English-language edition of *L'Osservatore Romano* (hereafter abbreviated OR), April 20, 2005, p. 3 (slightly modified translation).

At the Mass to mark the beginning of his pontificate, Pope Benedict XVI again emphasized the theme of joy in his description of the shepherd's task as one of imitating Christ's mission of seeking out the sheep that have strayed into the desert in order to lead them "towards the place of life, towards friendship with the Son of God, towards the One who gives us life, and life in abundance". The shepherd has the responsibility of feeding the sheep. To feed them means to love them and to be ready to suffer for and on account of them. Loving means "giving the sheep what is truly good, the nourishment of God's truth, of God's Word, the nourishment of his presence, which he gives us in the Blessed Sacrament". The purpose of the priest's life, the Pope concluded, is "to reveal God to men", and the pastoral ministry, in all its dimensions, is, ultimately, "a service to joy, to God's joy which longs to break into the world".[2]

The same note of joy marked the World Youth Day celebrations of August 2005 in Cologne. In an interview with Vatican Radio prior to his departure for the city on the Rhine, Pope Benedict expressed the hope that the young pilgrims who gathered there would discover above all the joy of being Christian.[3] Addressing the Roman Curia in December 2005, the Pope spoke of Eucharistic adoration, so much part of the Cologne celebrations, remarking that adoration is itself a source of joy.[4] Again, on an Advent pastoral visit to the Roman parish of Santa Maria Consolatrice, the titular church that had been assigned to him when

[2] Benedict XVI, Homily at the Mass for the inauguration of the Pontificate, April 24, 2005, in OR, April 27, 2005, pp. 8–9.

[3] See Benedict XVI, interview broadcast on Vatican Radio, August 15, 2005.

[4] See Benedict XVI, Address to the Roman Curia, December 22, 2005, in OR, January 4, 2006, p. 5.

he became a Cardinal in 1977, the Holy Father insisted that joy, which is motivated by the closeness and goodness of a loving God, is central to the Christian message. Commenting on the Gospel of the day, St. Luke's account of the Annunciation, he drew attention to the significance of the angel's greeting to Mary, "Rejoice!" (Lk 1:28), explaining that "the first word of the New Testament is an invitation to joy".[5]

Initially, this emphasis on joy appears somewhat surprising. Given the complexity and gravity of the world's problems and the challenges facing the Church in making the Christian message heard in a context of increasing secularization, it may seem that joy is somehow secondary, if not simply trivial. Yet, as Joseph Ratzinger's writings make clear, joy is crucial to the proclamation of the faith in today's world. Authentic joy is not something flippant, transient, or superficial, nor is it a mere feeling of euphoria that can be generated at will or by engaging in the various forms of pleasure or entertainment that today's world has to offer. Rather, it is an abiding God-given reality, a "fruit of the Holy Spirit" (see Gal 5:22), characterized by profound serenity and inner peace, which flows from allowing oneself to be embraced by God's love and is capable of withstanding all the trials and tribulations of life. Joy, like love, is at the heart of what it means to be Christian, and it testifies to the conviction that human life has an ultimate meaning revealed to us by God and guaranteed by his unfailing love. The Christian message, the gospel or "glad tidings", reveals the path to the lasting joy that satisfies the deepest needs of the human heart.

[5] Benedict XVI, Homily at the Mass for the Fourth Sunday of Advent, December 18, 2005, in OR, January 4, 2006, p. 11. On the translation of Lk 1:28, see below, p. 39.

This book is dedicated to the theme of joy in the thought of Joseph Ratzinger, now Pope Benedict XVI.[6] For an adequate discussion of this theme, it does not suffice to formulate a synthesis of the texts where he speaks explicitly of joy. Christian joy is comprehensible only on the basis of the fundamental revealed truths about the Triune God and about man, whom God creates, redeems, sanctifies, and intends for a life of eternal joy. Genuine and full acceptance of these truths and a sharing through God's grace in the life of the Blessed Trinity make authentic joy possible.

The first chapter sets the context for Joseph Ratzinger's reflections on joy. It shows how contemporary man, who is afflicted by so many fears and anxieties, is in need of hearing once again the Christian message of joy. Particular attention is devoted to the phenomena of boredom, spiritual lethargy or acedia, and the sense of meaninglessness that affect many of our contemporaries. To overcome these negative realities, it is necessary to promote a culture of joy. To do so, one must turn to the gospel, which indicates the path to the true joy that the world so badly needs.

For Joseph Ratzinger, joy is dependent on truth and love: authentic joy arises from man's experiencing and accepting God's love for him and from the saving truth he has revealed to him. St. Augustine, whose thought is a major influence on Ratzinger's, speaks in his *Confessions* of the joy that arises from the truth, *gaudium de veritate* (10, 23, 33). In chapter 2, the connection between joy and truth is explored, with special reference to Ratzinger's writings on truth and

[6] For a brief treatment of this theme, see also Bruno Le Pivain, "*Gaudium de Veritate*: aux sources de la joie véritable", in *Kephas* 17 (2006): 45–55. This number of *Kephas* contains a useful series of articles on various aspects of Pope Benedict's thought.

relativism in the context of world religions and reductive theories about reason's capabilities. Chapter 3 is concerned with the experience of a grace-filled Christian life, which is a sharing in the life of God himself and which manifests itself in the possession of the three primary supernatural attitudes or theological virtues of faith, hope, and love (or charity). Such a life, lived in fidelity to the truth and in accordance with these virtues, gives rise to enduring joy.

Authentic Christian living is a sharing in the life of the Blessed Trinity. Chapter 4 deals with the specific Christian understanding of God in the light of the biblical revelation of God as personal and as Trinity. God, though transcendent, reveals himself as close to man, as one who can be invoked in prayer and in whom man can place his trust. This is motive for deep joy. Furthermore, the revelation of the mystery of the Trinity shows how the category of relatedness is fundamental to the understanding of reality. The self-giving love characteristic of God's life provides a model for human living, and our sharing in the life of the Trinity through God's grace makes it possible for us to live a loving, fulfilled, and joyful life.

Chapter 5 turns to the theme of creation, which Joseph Ratzinger sees as the key to a correct understanding of who man is. Since the doctrine of creation has consequences for ethics and worship, he regards it as providing direction for human life. Chapter 6 is concerned with the person and saving work of Jesus Christ. Christ's intimate relation to the Father, expressed in constant prayer, and his redemptive work on the Cross, which brings about our salvation, have much to teach about the nature of Christian prayer and liturgy. Chapter 7 is devoted to the Holy

Spirit, the "Spirit of eternal joy",[7] promised by Christ to
the disciples and poured out upon them in order to lead
them to the fullness of the truth, build up the Church,
and bring people into intimate union with God.

The eighth chapter is concerned with the Church's essential nature and her mission to maintain the spirit of joy in
the world, and to bring people into contact with the joy
that gives meaning to their lives. Christ makes available to
the Church the supreme gift of his own Eucharistic presence, which gives people the opportunity to grow in joy
and friendship with the Lord in a unique and privileged
way; this is the theme of the ninth chapter.

All of this might give the impression that joy is something that is easy to acquire and maintain. However, even
the faithful Christian, who lives a holy life in fidelity to the
truth and in a spirit of love for God and neighbor, continually faces all kinds of obstacles on the path of life. Apart
from the disappointment and incomprehension that he may
regularly encounter, he must also face up to suffering and
death, which represent the supreme challenge to his happiness in this life. Chapter 10 asks whether it is possible to
rejoice in the face of these painful realities. The final chapter shows how eternal life is a motive for joy, not only as a
promise of eternal happiness, but also as a present reality
shaping our way of living now in this earthly life.

Although this book refers on occasion to what Joseph Ratzinger has written or said following his election as successor

---

[7] Joseph Ratzinger, *Der Gott Jesu Christi: Betrachtungen über den Dreieinigen
Gott* (Munich: Kösel, 2006), p. 188. This book was originally published in
1976, and an English translation, entitled *The God of Jesus Christ: Meditations
on God in the Trinity*, was published by Franciscan Herald Press in 1978. A
reprint is in preparation by Ignatius Press.

of Peter, for the most part it is based on his theological, spiritual, and pastoral writings as professor in various German universities (Bonn, Münster, Tübingen, and Regensburg) and later as Archbishop of Munich and Prefect of the Congregation for the Doctrine of the Faith. A deeper understanding of Pope Benedict's Magisterium requires constant reference to his earlier writings, in which the same themes are treated in considerable depth, in the light of Scripture and the Church's tradition and in dialogue with contemporary concerns. In this regard, it may prove both useful and illuminating to say something about the kind of theological reflection we shall encounter in the course of this book. Although the list is certainly incomplete, a number of characteristics come to mind:

1. All of Joseph Ratzinger's writings are solidly *scriptural*. Scripture is, of course, the soul of all theology,[8] but not all theologians make such widespread use of Scripture as the primary source and inspiration of their reflections as Ratzinger does. While he makes judicious use of the most reliable findings of modern exegesis, he is careful to read Scripture within the tradition of the Church and as a unity, centered on the person and saving work of Jesus Christ.

2. Ratzinger's work is also firmly grounded in *tradition*, for he is convinced that the truth gradually unfolds itself in the life of the Church under the direction of the Holy Spirit

[8] See Second Vatican Council, Decree on Priestly Training, *Optatam Totius*, October 28, 1965, no. 16. For Joseph Ratzinger's approach to scriptural exegesis, see the Erasmus lecture "Biblical Interpretation in Crisis: On the Question of the Foundations and Approaches of Exegesis Today", which he delivered on January 27, 1988 in St. Peter's Church, New York, in *The Essential Pope Benedict XVI: His Central Writings and Speeches*, ed. John F. Thornton and Susan B. Varenne (San Francisco: HarperSanFrancisco, 2007), pp. 243–58.

(cf. Jn 16:13).[9] His theology is shaped by long familiarity with the Fathers of the Church, especially St. Augustine, whose understanding of the Church was the subject of his doctoral thesis *People of God and House of God in St. Augustine's Doctrine of the Church*, defended in 1951 and first published in 1954.[10]

3. Joseph Ratzinger's approach to the various issues dealt with in his writings is characterized above all by a search for the *truth*. He does not seek originality for originality's sake, but is convinced that the resources of Scripture and tradition provide the fundamental orientation guiding our attempts to answer contemporary questions and challenges concerning the faith. Acceptance of the faith in its entirety as the truth that we have received from God and that is taught by the Church, over which we are not the masters, is the precondition for any fruitful theological work.[11] This attitude of receptivity does not reduce theology to a mindless repetition of past insights and conclusions. Theology becomes an exciting and fruitful pursuit when the theologian bases his work on the pluralism in unity found in the Old and New Testaments, and the Church's teaching, while keeping in mind the ongoing life of faith. There is a unity in faith but a

[9] On this point, see especially Second Vatican Council, Dogmatic Constitution on Divine Revelation, *Dei Verbum*, November 18, 1965, no. 8.

[10] Joseph Ratzinger, *Volk und Haus Gottes in Augustins Lehre von der Kirche* (Munich: Zink, 1954); unamended reprint with a new preface (St. Ottilien: EOS Verlag, 1992). To date, this work has not been translated into English. It has been translated into Italian as *Popolo e casa di Dio in Sant'Agostino* (Milan: Jaca Book, 1978).

[11] Joseph Ratzinger has explored the nature of theology in various writings; see, for example, *The Nature and Mission of Theology: Approaches to Understanding Its Role in the Light of Present Controversy* (San Francisco: Ignatius Press, 1995); "Faith and Theology", in *Pilgrim Fellowship of Faith: The Church as Communion* (San Francisco: Ignatius Press, 2005), pp. 17–28; "What in Fact Is Theology", in *Pilgrim Fellowship of Faith*, pp. 29–37.

plurality in theology; indeed, the fixing of a common reference point in the truth of Christian faith makes plurality possible. A legitimate theological pluralism arises "not when we make it the object of our desire, but when everyone wants the truth with all his power and in his own epoch".[12]

4. The foregoing points make it clear that Joseph Ratzinger's theology is profoundly *ecclesial*. It is in the Church that we encounter Christ: she is our "contemporaneity with Christ: there is no other".[13] It is within the communion of the Church that the Holy Spirit leads us into the fullness of truth. For this reason, the Church is not an authority that remains foreign to the scientific character of theological reflection, but the ground of theology's existence and the condition that makes it possible.[14] Indeed, as the German exegete Heinrich Schlier, then a member of the Confessing Evangelical Church, reminded his listeners in 1935, at the height of the Nazi campaign to make the Church an instrument of its own policies, "care for the Word of God among men is entrusted to the Church alone".[15] The teaching office of the Church is not above the Word of God but exercises a humble service to it: this ecclesial office has the task of ensuring that Scripture is not manipulated and that its clear meaning is preserved from the conflict of hypotheses.[16] The freedom of theology is its bond with the Church and any other freedom "is a betrayal both of itself and of the object entrusted to it".[17]

[12] Ratzinger, *The Nature and Mission of Theology*, p. 97.

[13] Ibid., p. 60.

[14] See ibid., p. 61.

[15] Heinrich Schlier, "Die Verantwortung der Kirche für den theologischen Unterricht", in his *Der Geist und die Kirche*, ed. V. Kubina and K. Lehmann (Freiburg im Breisgau: Herder, 1980), p. 241, as quoted by Ratzinger in *The Nature and Mission of Theology*, p. 45.

[16] See Ratzinger, *Pilgrim Fellowship of Faith*, p. 35.

[17] Ratzinger, *The Nature and Mission of Theology*, p. 46.

Divorced from the faith of the Church, theological reflection
would become no more than a personal theory or, at best, a
philosophy of religion. It would also run the risk of being
reduced to no more than an alternative formulation of the
fashionable ideas shaping contemporary popular culture or
of falling prey to political or commercial interests. Such speculation on religion could well be interesting, but it is hardly
what one would stake one's life on.

5. The writings of Joseph Ratzinger are marked by a
certain *fragmentary* quality, in the sense that he never produced a complete synthesis of the Christian faith and that
many of his writings, being occasional pieces, do not fully
develop the profound intuitions that he enunciates. In part,
this is in keeping with his insistence that the faith is not a
system but a path, along which we travel together in the
communion of the Church toward the fullness of truth. It
is also due to the simple fact that he had to give up his
preferred life as an academic to serve the Church first as
Archbishop of Munich, then as Prefect of the Congregation of the Doctrine of the Faith, and now, of course, as
Pope. Ratzinger is well aware of the unfinished character
of much of his writing, yet, as his former student Vincent
Twomey points out, "He makes a virtue out of this 'weakness'" and presents his various writings as "contributions
to an ongoing debate".[18]

6. Despite the admittedly incomplete nature of much of
Ratzinger's work, there is an *inner consistency* that marks
all of his writings, although each piece "never fails to

[18] D. Vincent Twomey, *Pope Benedict XVI: The Conscience of Our Age. A
Theological Portrait* (San Francisco: Ignatius Press, 2007), p. 41; also his "The
Mind of Benedict XVI", in *Claremont Review of Books* 5 (2005): 66. Chapter 2 of Twomey's book, which expands his *Claremont Review* article, provides a useful overview of Joseph Ratzinger's writings over the years.

surprise with its freshness, originality, and depth." [19] Many
of his basic intuitions about the nature of the Church, the
relation of Church and State, the place of history in Christian thinking, and the distinction between utopia and eschatology (with its consequences for the theology of politics
and liberation theology) may be traced back to his doctoral thesis on St. Augustine and his *Habilitationsschrift*
(or postdoctoral research required for university teaching)
entitled *The Theology of History in St. Bonaventure*, defended
in 1957 and first published in 1959.[20] With regard to the
inner unity of Ratzinger's theology, an excellent starting
point for delving into his rich and exciting work is his
Introduction to Christianity.[21] This book, first published in
1968, was based on a series of lectures on the Apostles'
Creed that he gave in the summer term of 1967 at the
University of Tübingen to students of all faculties. It opens
"with a masterly attempt to situate the question of belief
and its communal expression in the modern world before
going on to comment on the contents of the Creed".[22]
Many of the issues that receive more detailed treatment in

[19] Twomey, *Pope Benedict XVI*, p. 42.

[20] On the difficulties encountered with regard to his *Habilitationsschrift*, see
Joseph Ratzinger's own account in his *Milestones: Memoirs 1927–1977* (San
Francisco: Ignatius Press, 1998), pp. 103–14. Ratzinger's *Habilitationsschrift* was
translated into English as *The Theology of History in St. Bonaventure* (Chicago:
Franciscan Herald Press, 1971).

[21] The first English edition of *Introduction to Christianity*, translated by J. R.
Foster, was published in London in 1969 and in New York in 1970 and
reprinted by Ignatius Press in 1990. I refer to the second edition published
by Ignatius Press in 2004. This edition is almost identical in content to the
original, with some corrections to the translation and the addition of a new
preface, written in 2000 by the then Cardinal Ratzinger, entitled "*Introduction to Christianity*: Yesterday, Today, Tomorrow", which surveys some of the
new challenges to the Christian faith that have emerged since 1968.

[22] Twomey, "The Mind of Benedict XVI", p. 67.

his later writings make their appearance here: the relationship between faith and reason, the consequences of the
doctrine of creation for our understanding of the human
person, the interpretation of Scripture, ecumenism, cate-
chetics, the Eucharist, the nature of Christian worship, and
eschatology.

7. Ratzinger's is a theology of *dialogue*, sensitive to contemporary questions. As is clear from *Introduction to Christianity*, his theology does not limit itself to an orthodox
reaffirmation of the central tenets of the faith. His method
involves listening to the discussions and frequently implicit
questions of modern culture and contemporary theological scholarship in order to uncover whatever truths they
may contain and respond in the light of faith. In this way,
his theology is not an abstract speculation with little to say
to modern man, but is solidly connected with the experience of people today: he shows how perennial Christian
truths are relevant to our questioning and illuminate the
path for life's journey. Emblematic of his respectful approach
to the positions of others is his attitude to the role played
by heresies in the development of Christian dogma. After
surveying the heresies that arose in the course of the Church's
formulation of the Trinitarian dogma, he points out that
they should not be viewed simply as failures of human
thought in reflecting upon the ineffable. Rather, "every
heresy is at the same time the cipher for an abiding truth,
a cipher we must now preserve with other simultaneously
valid statements, separated from which it produces a false
impression." [23]

8. It is clear from the foregoing that Joseph Ratzinger's
theology is eminently *pastoral*. Apart from writings explicitly

---

[23] Ratzinger, *Introduction to Christianity*, 2nd ed., p. 173.

devoted to pastoral themes such as preaching,[24] the celebration of the liturgy,[25] catechesis,[26] ethics,[27] and the Christian
approach to politics,[28] most of his theological output is produced with an eye to practical questions about living the

---

[24] Ratzinger's theoretical work on preaching is *Dogma und Verkündigung*
(Munich and Freiburg in Breisgau: Erich Wewel Verlag, 1973), only partially
translated into English as *Dogma and Preaching* (Chicago: Franciscan Herald
Press, 1985). Various collections of his homilies and meditations have been
published, including *Vom Sinn des Christseins: Drei Adventspredigten* (Munich:
Kösel, 2005), originally published in 1965; *Die Hoffnung des Senfkorns* (Meitingen and Freising: Kyrios Verlag, 1973); *Gottes Glanz in unserer Zeit: Medi-
tationen zum Kirchenjahr* (Freiburg im Breisgau: Herder, 2005); *Der Segen der
Weihnacht Meditationen* (Freiburg im Breisgau: Herder, 2005); *Komm Heiliger
Geist! Pfingtspredigten*, 2nd ed. (Munich: Erich Wewel Verlag, 2005). In English
translation: *Seek That Which Is Above* (San Francisco: Ignatius Press, 1986, 2007);
What It Means to Be a Christian (San Francisco: Ignatius Press, 2006); *Images
of Hope: Meditations on Major Feasts* (San Francisco: Ignatius Press, 2006); *The
Blessing of Christmas* (San Francisco: Ignatius Press, 2007).

[25] In this regard, one should mention above all his trilogy on the liturgy:
The Feast of Faith: Approaches to a Theology of the Liturgy (San Francisco: Ignatius
Press, 1986); *A New Song for the Lord: Faith in Christ and Liturgy* (New York:
Crossroad, 1996); *The Spirit of the Liturgy* (San Francisco: Ignatius Press, 2000).

[26] See, for example, Joseph Ratzinger, *Introduction to the Catechism of the
Catholic Church*, with Christoph Schönborn (San Francisco: Ignatius Press,
1994); Joseph Ratzinger, *Gospel, Catechesis, Catechism: Sidelights on the Catechism of the Catholic Church* (San Francisco: Ignatius Press, 1997). Particularly
significant is Joseph Ratzinger's lecture on the contemporary state of catechesis, delivered in January 1983 in Paris and Lyons, which is published in
English as "Handing on the Faith and the Sources of the Faith", in Joseph
Ratzinger et al., *Handing on the Faith in an Age of Disbelief* (San Francisco:
Ignatius Press, 2006), pp. 13–40.

[27] See, for example, "The Church's Teaching Authority—Faith—Morals",
in Joseph Ratzinger et al., *Principles of Christian Morality* (San Francisco: Ignatius Press, 1986); Joseph Ratzinger, *La via della fede: Le ragioni dell'etica nell'epoca
presente* (Milan: Ares, 1996); Joseph Ratzinger, "Conscience and Truth", in
Crisis of Conscience, ed. John M. Haas (New York: Crossroad, 1996), pp. 1–20.

[28] See, for example, the following by Joseph Ratzinger: *Church, Ecumenism
and Politics: New Essays in Ecclesiology* (Slough: St. Paul Publications, 1988);
Wahrheit, Werte, Macht: Prüfsteine der pluralistischen Gesellschaft (Freiburg im Breisgau: Herder, 1993); *A Turning Point for Europe* (San Francisco: Ignatius Press,

faith in the contemporary world in the face of increasing
secularization and religious pluralism. The pastoral approach
does not mean accommodation to current ways of thinking
and behaving, but entails bringing the joy and the light of
the truth to bear on contemporary situations in a manner
that is convincing and sensitive to the questions of modern
man. In this regard, Ratzinger cites an entry from the diary
of Romano Guardini, which could easily apply to himself:
"Truth has such a clear and calm power. My aim in pastoral
work is this: to help by the power of the truth." [29]

9. While Joseph Ratzinger has published some explicitly
spiritual writings, such as the retreat he gave to the Roman
Curia in 1983,[30] and the one he gave to priest members of
Comunione e Liberazione in 1986,[31] as well as his contribution to the development of a spiritual Christology, *Behold
the Pierced One*,[32] his writings on priestly spirituality,[33] and
the magnificent chapter on the Lord's Prayer in his first book
written as Pope, *Jesus of Nazareth*,[34] all of his theology is

1994); *Christianity and the Crisis of Cultures* (San Francisco: Ignatius Press,
2006); *Values in a Time of Upheaval* (New York: Crossroad; San Francisco:
Ignatius Press, 2006).

[29] The diary entry is dated February 28, 1954; see Romano Guardini,
Wahrheit des Denkens und Wahrheit des Tuns, 3rd ed. (Paderborn: Schöningh,
1980), p. 85; Ratzinger, *The Nature and Mission of Theology*, p. 92, n. 20.

[30] See Joseph Ratzinger, *Journey towards Easter: Retreat Given in the Vatican
in the Presence of Pope John Paul II* (Slough: St. Paul Publications, 1987).

[31] See Joseph Ratzinger, *The Yes of Jesus Christ: Spiritual Exercises in Faith,
Hope and Love* (New York: Crossroad, 2005), originally published as *To Look
on Christ: Exercises in Faith, Hope and Love* (New York: Crossroad, 1991).

[32] Joseph Ratzinger, *Behold the Pierced One: An Approach to a Spiritual Christology* (San Francisco: Ignatius Press, 1986).

[33] See Joseph Ratzinger, *Ministers of Your Joy: Meditations on Priestly Spirituality* (Slough: St. Paul Publications, 1989).

[34] Joseph Ratzinger (Pope Benedict XVI), *Jesus of Nazareth: From the Baptism in the Jordan to the Transfiguration* (New York: Doubleday, 2007), pp. 128–68.

characterized by a strong *spiritual and prayerful* note. It is
no exaggeration to say that just as his explicitly spiritual
writings are profoundly theological, so too his theological-
cal writings are deeply spiritual and indeed lead to prayer.
In this regard, his writings remind one of the theological
method of Hans Urs von Balthasar or the objective approach
to spiritual theology found in the writings of Blessed
Columba Marmion, an author with whom, more than likely,
he would have been well acquainted in the seminary. However, it is probably even more true to say that his theology
reflects his long familiarity with the Church Fathers, who
did not separate theological reflection from prayer and pastoral concerns.

10. A final characteristic of Joseph Ratzinger's theology is the sheer *joy in the faith* that it exudes. Overcoming
a narrow moralistic and legalistic interpretation of Christianity, Ratzinger emphasizes that Christian faith is not
a burden but brings joy to the heart of man. For Ratzinger, joy emerges from the totality of Christian faith
when it is received in an open and generous heart. Joy
is an overarching or synthesizing theme in his writings.
It refers both to God's gifts of love, salvation, and eternal
life and to man's response, shaped by the supernatural
attitudes of faith, hope, and charity and lived out amid
life's joys and sorrows in the community of the Church
as she journeys toward the definitive encounter with her
Lord.

Joseph Ratzinger was once asked to describe what he
saw as specific to his theology and way of doing theology.
In his reply, which synthesizes many of the points made
above, he explains that he has always consciously pursued a
theology firmly grounded in the faith of the Church and in
dialogue with contemporary thought:

I began with the theme of the Church, and it is present in everything. Only, in dealing with the Church it was important to me, and it has become increasingly important, that the Church not be an end in herself but exist so that God may be seen. In that respect I would say that I study the theme of the Church with the intention of opening a vista onto God. And in this sense God is the real central theme of my endeavors.

I have never tried to create a system of my own, an individual theology. What is specific, if you want to call it that, is that I simply want to think in communion with the faith of the Church, and that means above all to think in communion with the great thinkers of the faith. The aim is not an isolated theology that I draw out of myself but one that opens as widely as possible into the common intellectual pathway of the faith. For this reason exegesis was always very important. I couldn't imagine a purely philosophical theology. The point of departure is first of all the Word. That we believe the word of God, that we try really to get to know and understand it and then, as I said, to think it together with the great masters of the faith. This gives my theology a somewhat biblical character and also bears the stamp of the Fathers, especially Augustine. But it goes without saying that I try not to stop with the ancient Church but to hold fast to the great high points of thought and at the same time to bring contemporary thought into the discussion.[35]

An attempt, such as this, to convey something of the richness of the thought of Joseph Ratzinger, now Pope Benedict XVI, cannot hope to say everything. It is intended in the first place as an expression of gratitude for all that this

[35] Joseph Ratzinger, *Salt of the Earth: Christianity and the Catholic Church at the End of the Millennium, An Interview with Peter Seewald* (San Francisco: Ignatius Press, 1997), pp. 65–66.

author has gained over the years from frequenting Ratzinger's extraordinarily profound, inspiring, and wide-
ranging theological works. Incomplete and imperfect though
it is, this exploration of the central theme of joy also aims
at serving the Holy Father's message. It is hoped that these
pages will encourage the reader to engage Pope Benedict's
own writings and so come to know better the beauty and
joy of the Christian faith and grow in love of God and
neighbor.

Chapter I

A WORLD IN NEED OF JOY

At the outset, it could be objected that for many Christianity is anything but joyful. All too often it is perceived as a narrow system of duties and obligations, marked by legalism and scrupulosity, and forbidding what makes life enjoyable. Joseph Ratzinger is well aware that the perceived opposition of Christianity to joy is more likely to be advanced as a reason for leaving the Church than the various theoretical objections that can be raised against the faith.[1]

Among the representatives of this viewpoint, Ratzinger singles out the positions of the German anti-theist thinker Friedrich Nietzsche (1844–1900) as particularly significant.[2] Affirming the values of life and the realities of the world in which we live, Nietzsche saw Christian morality,

[1] See the following by Joseph Ratzinger: "Faith as Trust and Joy—Evangelium", in *Principles of Catholic Theology* (San Francisco: Ignatius Press, 1987), p. 76; *The Yes of Jesus Christ: Spiritual Exercises in Faith, Hope and Love* (New York: Crossroad, 2005), p. 72.

[2] For overviews of Nietzsche's thought, see Henri de Lubac, *The Drama of Atheist Humanism* (San Francisco: Ignatius Press, 1995), pp. 42–95; Martin Henry, *On Not Understanding God* (Dublin: Columba Press, 1997), pp. 224–59; William R. Schroeder, *Continental Philosophy: A Critical Approach* (Oxford: Blackwell, 2005), pp. 117–48.

19

with its emphasis on the heavenly kingdom, as a "capital crime against life", a denial of this world's joys.[3] As Pope Benedict XVI recalls in his encyclical *Deus Caritas Est*, Nietzsche accused Christianity, among other things, of having rejected human love or eros in favor of a new and exclusive vision of love expressed by the term *agape*:

> According to Friedrich Nietzsche, Christianity has poisoned *eros*, which for its part, while not completely succumbing, gradually degenerated into vice. Here the German philosopher was expressing a widely-held perception: doesn't the Church, with all her commandments and prohibitions, turn to bitterness the most precious thing in life? Doesn't she blow the whistle just when the joy which is the Creator's gift offers us a happiness which is itself a certain foretaste of the divine?[4]

Nietzsche had abandoned Christianity in his youth, and his hostility to it gradually became more and more explicit, culminating in his final work, the posthumously published *Ecce Homo* (written in 1888). Here, his rejection of the Christian faith is expressed in terms of the opposition of the emblematic figures of the Greek god Dionysus and the Crucified One.

Dionysus makes his first appearance in *The Birth of Tragedy* (1872), where he is invoked along with the god Apollo to illustrate how both life and art are informed by two principles, which Nietzsche terms the Dionysian and the Apollonian. Dionysus is the symbol of the stream of life

[3] Friedrich Nietzsche, *Der Wille zur Macht*, in *Werke*, vol. 15 (Leipzig: Alfred Kröner, 1899–), p. 327; cf. Benedict XVI, Address to the Clergy of the Diocese of Rome, March 2, 2006, in OR, March 15, 2006, p. 5.

[4] Benedict XVI, Encyclical Letter *Deus Caritas Est*, December 25, 2005, no. 3 (Vatican City: Libreria Editrice Vaticána, 2006).

itself. The Dionysian principle is associated with drunken ecstasy, which entails a breaking down of all barriers and an ignoring of all restraints, in order to bring about a union with the grandeur of life itself. The Apollonian principle emphasizes the notions of form, order, balance, and harmony. Life and art embody both principles: "Sometimes people discover a joy in existing that results from ecstatic immersion in the life-process; sometimes life transmutes itself by revealing a crystalline and geometric face." [5] At this point in Nietzsche's career, despite his marked predilection for Dionysus, it is not yet possible to determine which, if any, of the two will triumph over the other.[6]

With the passage of time, Nietzsche's opposition to Christianity would gradually become more violent and frantic. In later works, such as *Human, All Too Human* (1878–1880), *The Gay Science* (1882), *Thus Spoke Zarathustra* (1883–1885), *Beyond Good and Evil* (1886), and *Genealogy of Morals* (1887), Nietzsche proclaimed the "death of God" as the necessary condition for human flourishing and engaged in a sustained and multipronged attack on Christian morality.[7] Convinced that traditional religious beliefs and moral codes were no longer tenable and wishing to circumvent the foreseeable nihilist consequences of their collapse, he sought to promote a vision of man more conducive to the enhancement of life.

In *Beyond Good and Evil* and, more systematically, in *Genealogy of Morals* he describes the traditional ethical viewpoint as a "slave morality" created by weak-willed, incapable, and

---

[5] Schroeder, *Continental Philosophy*, p. 133.

[6] See de Lubac, *The Drama of Atheist Humanism*, p. 77.

[7] See Schroeder, *Continental Philosophy*, pp. 124–30.

unsuccessful people, who are ill-suited to life. Such people react against talented, assertive, and strong individuals, who embody what Nietzsche calls "master morality", whose proponents value whatever produces joy or delight, affirms life, and improves their capacity to live well. The virtues of the strong include pride, strength, passion, power, and exuberance. The strong evaluate things in terms of good and bad, where "bad" has no moral overtones, but simply denotes what is unhealthy or self-destructive.

Nietzsche surmises that specifically moral forms of goodness and virtue arose when the priests who ministered to unsuccessful and resentful slavish types simply inverted the standards of value and taught that the virtues of the strong and healthy are in fact "evil". Instead, they insist that goodness is to be found in weakness, humility, suffering, passivity, resignation, and self-denial. Nietzsche protests that such values impede the realization of the highest human possibilities and, as such, are opposed to whatever is truly life-affirming. For this reason, he sees Christianity as nothing more than an expression of the resentment, characteristic of the slave morality, against the aristocratic and strong, and, in the final analysis, a disaster for humanity.

To overcome the slave morality that hinders the full development of man's creative energies, Nietzsche insists that new modes of evaluation, connected with the morality of the strong, must be promoted. For Nietzsche, as for some late nineteenth-century French psychiatrists who coined the expression *la maladie catholique*, Christian morality, with its emphasis on authority and purity, produces rigid individuals who are weak, submissive, tortured in conscience, and incapable of self-development.[8] The Christian concept of

---

[8] See Ratzinger, "Faith as Trust and Joy", p. 77.

value must be rejected, he thunders, because, as his Zarathustra says, "We do not want to enter the kingdom of
heaven. We have become men—and so we want the kingdom of earth." [9]

In the autobiographical *Ecce Homo*, where Nietzsche offers
a retrospective examination of his entire corpus and describes
himself as a follower of Dionysus, he continues his bitter
attack on Christianity, contrasting the Crucified One and
his virtues of the weak with the figure of Dionysus and the
morality of the strong, exemplified by the man who "makes
sport ingenuously ... of everything that has hitherto been
called holy, good, untouchable, divine".[10] Nietzsche's hope
was that Dionysus, the god of life's exuberance, would replace
Christ as the standard moral and cultural reference of the
future.

Although Nietzsche's positions are, admittedly, open to
various interpretations and have frequently been manipulated, there is no doubt that popularized versions of his ideas
have exercised considerable influence. The championing of
a morality of the strong, as advocated in *Ecce Homo*, would
be eagerly embraced by twentieth-century totalitarian
regimes, especially by Nazism. As Ratzinger puts it, Nietzsche anticipates in uncanny detail the morality of the later
concentration-camp guards, "a world peopled by the inhu-
man and violent who are a mystery even to themselves".[11]
Nietzsche's rejection of Christian morality and indeed of
the idea that there is any absolute and universal moral law
has penetrated many sectors of society. As evidenced today
by any newspaper stand, mankind has at this stage freed

---

[9] Nietzsche, *Also sprach Zarathustra*, in *Werke*, vol. 6, p. 459.

[10] Nietzsche, *Ecce Homo*, in *Werke*, vol. 15, p. 154.

[11] Ratzinger, "Faith as Trust and Joy", p. 77.

itself from *la maladie catholique*. The question is: Has it become
healthier? Has it become happier or more free?

Today, human happiness appears very fragile. Rather than
making possible the self-fulfillment that leads to joy, liberation from past restraints seems to have resulted in disillu-
sion, boredom, and even a certain disgust with life. Damage
to the environment, social upheaval, the breakdown of the
traditional family, the widespread "culture of death", international instability, and the terrorist threat of recent years
have all contributed to an increased unease, anxiety, and
fear about the future. In a world where many live as though
there were no God, there is a widespread perception that
life is without meaning and lacks direction. The various
surrogates of genuine love have left people dissatisfied and
disappointed. Yet love is a primordial reality, so deeply rooted
in the human heart that if the yearning for it is not satisfied, life itself is doomed to misery and comes to seem point-
less. To overcome the gnawing sense of despair, many take
refuge in a ceaseless activism, seek ever more varied forms
of communal or personal entertainment, or indulge in diverse
kinds of escapism.

Among the various symptoms of malaise in contemporary life, three are of particular interest to our theme, namely,
the chronic boredom that many experience, despite all that
life has to offer; the spiritual listlessness or acedia that afflicts
even Christians, who should have every reason to rejoice;
and the frequently unarticulated belief that life itself is without ultimate meaning.

1. Boredom

In a recent article, Michael Hanby, one of the original
contributors to the important volume of theological essays

Radical Orthodoxy,[12] provides a penetrating analysis of the phenomenon of boredom.[13] In it, he relates boredom to subjective dispositions and to a certain understanding of the world that is ultimately connected with philosophical nominalism and a voluntarist understanding of freedom. Hanby argues that all of these are factors contributing to what Pope John Paul II called the "culture of death", a "culture" that in recent years has manifested itself not only in the elimination of the unwanted but also in more terrifying ways in the sudden eruption of hitherto unthinkable violence with no apparent rationale. To overcome boredom and combat the culture of death, Hanby proposes that a culture of joy should be promoted. Such a culture, he argues, has an ultimate religious and transcendent foundation, for joy arises from recognizing the objective goodness of finite things, which reflect the love and goodness of the Creator.

Hanby begins by distinguishing boredom from its closely related antecedents, acedia and *ennui*, which he describes as forms of melancholy involving a moral and spiritual affront to a true and meaningful order of things. Boredom, however, points to a double failure of a different kind, "a failure of the world to be compelling to a subject ostensibly entitled to such an expectation *and* a failure or incapacity on the part of the subject to be compelled".[14] By "compelling", Hanby seems to be referring to the capacity of external objects to attract or draw the subject, a capacity that is based on their objective goodness. The twofold failure underlying boredom indicates that this pathology is closely

[12] John Milbank, Catherine Pickstock, and Graham Ward, eds., *Radical Orthodoxy: A New Theology* (London: Routledge, 1999).

[13] Michael Hanby, "The Culture of Death, the Ontology of Boredom, and the Resistance of Joy", in *Communio* (American ed.) 31 (2004): 181–99.

[14] Ibid., p. 184.

aligned with hopelessness. In today's society, it frequently manifests itself in forms of consumerist excess arising from the sense of helplessness that leads to a disinclination for social or political involvement.

The endemic boredom of a substantial part of the population is a major presupposition for the modern entertainment culture. Our lives are considered empty, unlivable, and meaningless without a constant stream of stimulation and distraction, a stream that is inevitably subject to the law of diminishing returns. Corresponding to the subject's sense of emptiness, the world too is regarded as devoid of form, objective beauty, or a true order of goods that naturally and of themselves would compel our interest. The result is, as Hanby says, that all choices can only be indifferently related to one another: none is intrinsically good or bad, and indeed no good approaches that of choice itself. As a result, most citizens of the modern West end up living fragmented lives, characterized by internal contradictions. Their choices are aimed less at pleasing than anesthetizing and distracting from an "empty existence imposed by a formless goalless world".[15]

Hanby connects the experience of boredom with the voluntarist notion of freedom (or freedom of indifference), which came to the fore in the late Middle Ages, largely due to the influence of William of Ockham, and is the dominant understanding of freedom in today's world. It contrasts with the more traditional scriptural and patristic notion, according to which freedom consists in living as one truly wishes, that is, in happiness. This kind of freedom, the so-called "freedom of quality" or "freedom for excellence", is rooted in the natural inclinations for truth and

[15] Ibid., p. 186.

goodness.[16] Consequently, it is in pursuing what is truly good that we become more free and truly happy. Ultimately, then, according to this understanding, freedom is dependent on our relationship to God, who is truth, goodness, and love.

This notion of freedom has been displaced in modern times by the voluntarist "freedom of indifference". Voluntarist freedom sees the natural inclinations as a hindrance rather than a foundation for freedom, and free choice is understood merely as a capacity to choose indifferently between contraries. Finite things, previously seen as objectively true and good, and thus as capable of exercising an attraction in line with the subject's inclinations toward truth and goodness, are now seen merely as possible objects on which the subject's choice can indifferently bear. Furthermore, individual choices are seen in an atomized way, exercising no influence on subsequent choices. Voluntarist freedom thus remains unaffected by our choices, whether these be good or evil. Hanby argues that it is this notion of freedom that has produced the endemic boredom of modern society, which, in turn, has led to the negation of real freedom itself (for Hanby, real freedom is not voluntarist freedom but the more traditional freedom for excellence):

It is the malaise of boredom, and not the will to power or pleasure, that is the full-flower of the voluntarism at the root of the culture of death, because it is boredom that

[16] On these understandings of freedom, see Servais Pinckaers, *The Sources of Christian Ethics* (Washington, D.C.: Catholic University of America Press, 1995), pp. 327–99. On the link between voluntarist freedom and the culture of death, see John Paul II, *Evangelium Vitae*, March 25, 1995, nos. 19–20. For Joseph Ratzinger's understanding of freedom, see "Freedom and Truth", in *Truth and Tolerance: Christian Belief and World Religions* (San Francisco: Ignatius Press, 2004), pp. 231–58.

finally completes voluntarism's nominalist project of denying the compulsion of transcendental beauty, goodness and
truth in the mediation of particular finite forms. In boredom, in our indifference to the vast array of numbingly
different choices, we see not only the nominalistic evacuation of finite form, but the evacuation of both the desire
ordered to and dependent upon that form and the self-gift
compelled by its claims upon our desire. This is to say, iron-
ically, that it is only in boredom that we see voluntaristic
freedom finally negating itself.[17]

True freedom is not the only thing that is lost. As Hanby
goes on to argue, a world "beyond good and evil", in which
nothing is regarded as either genuinely good or genuinely
bad, and no truth, goodness, or beauty is perceived in our
experience of finite things, is one in which nothing is either
intrinsically desirable or detestable. In such a world, nothing can be regarded as holy. Boredom, then, is "the defining condition of a people uniquely in danger of losing their
capacity to love", of failing to grasp the mystery of their
own being and of losing their very humanity.[18]

Such a danger is clearly inherent in the culture of death,
which is obsessed with programming, controlling, and dom-
inating birth and death, since it has evacuated human life of
all intrinsic meaning in favor of a purely utilitarian understanding in terms of social and economic efficiency. The culture of death, Hanby maintains, is not the result of hedonistic
excess but arises from the sense of hopelessness and despair
intrinsic to a world of boredom and, especially in its recent
more violent manifestations, is perceived as providing an escape
from them; it is, therefore, "the poison fruit, excessive despair,

[17] Hanby, "The Culture of Death", p. 187.
[18] Ibid., pp. 187–88; cf. John Paul II, *Evangelium Vitae*, no. 22.

born of a world made boring by our 'freedom' and a freedom made deadly by our boredom".[19]

As mentioned earlier, Hanby argues that we need to promote a culture of joy in order to combat the culture of death. While boredom signals a failed relationship between the self and the world, joy, the simultaneous delight and rest in another, affirms that external objects possess a goodness and beauty, which, though pleasing to the subject, are not reducible to the subject's pleasure, precisely because they are objective. Consequently, "the cultivation of joy is essential if the reductive, instrumentalist view of reality underpinning the culture of death is to be resisted."[20] Joy must be distinguished from both the escapist pleasure of the consumer economy and the exploitation that increasingly marks the human relationships formed by that economy. It presupposes relation and is responsive to the prompting of another. It implies both giving and receiving, the self-gift and loss and repose of oneself in the compelling goodness and beauty of another. Joy is unintelligible apart from love; it is the fruit of love's enduring embrace. Finite human joy and love point to a higher love beyond them:

> Love, as simultaneous self-gift and desire, is only intelligible as moved by goodness, and the very act, in loving, in simultaneously desiring and giving, affirms the independent goodness of the beloved and allows the beloved simply to be unto itself, precisely in being embraced. So joy, as the fruit of love, performs a judgment about the world beyond the lover, and yet this judgment can only be true, the beloved can only genuinely *be* good, if indeed it mediates a goodness and reveals a beauty that transcends it, that is, if it is

[19] Hanby, "The Culture of Death", p. 192.
[20] Ibid., p. 193.

itself the fruit of a love which in loving, bestows diffusive goodness upon it in its very specificity. Both love and joy presuppose the prior claims of beauty and goodness, and the reality of finite beauty and goodness are finally dependent upon a higher love not their own.[21]

The ultimate foundation for joy, as Hanby recognizes, is the Blessed Trinity. From the beginning, the world is created "very good" (Gen 1:31). The Resurrection of Christ, apart from manifesting the Father's delight in the Son, also glorifies creation, elevating it into the eternal Sabbath of God's own delight. Joy somehow overcomes the opposition between act and repose, since wherever work is moved by delight in its products, rest is incorporated into its very structure. In this sense, joy both affirms and participates in the eternal and transcendent:

> God himself is joy: the good of all goodness, the perfect coincidence of giving and receiving, and the perfection of delight, beyond beginning, goal or end. As Trinity God is both perfect act and perfect rest, and is each "because" he is the other. It is this that is the source of any claim creation has to real goodness, and this that every instance of true joy presupposes and affirms.[22]

While love between humans, especially when ordered to the worship of God himself, most closely approximates that joy, joy itself is not restricted to describing the fruit of love between persons. Since finite forms are in principle capable of revealing something of God's infinite wisdom and goodness, and thus of eliciting our affection and affording us rest, then, in various degrees of closeness to God, the

[21] Ibid., pp. 195–96.
[22] Ibid., pp. 196–97.

divine archetype, all genuine joy or delight that recognizes
intrinsic goodness will reflect Trinitarian bliss.

A culture of joy is based on these truths and pays particular attention to the production of both material forms and
forms of life in which the transcendent commitments inte-
gral to joy and to human activity can flourish. Joy, with its
delight in the intrinsic, its commitment to the transcendent
and its repose in the transcendent through its embrace of
finite form, is "absolutely essential to the good order and to
the genuine letting be of any properly human activity, and
indeed proper human being".[23] Such a culture knows how
to celebrate and to pray, and only such a culture will be
capable of great art and of sustaining marriage, rearing children, and fulfilling the natural obligation between generations in caring for the sick and the dying. This is the kind of
culture that is capable of resisting the corrosive forces of the
culture of death and of making genuine freedom possible.

Hanby advocates a culture of joy that is intimately connected with love and truth, and is ultimately rooted in the
communion of the Blessed Trinity. Joseph Ratzinger, whose
explorations into the roots of joy predate Hanby's, arrives
at similar conclusions, particularly in his discussions on acedia and meaninglessness.

2. Acedia

Acedia (*acidia*), or "sloth", is a far more serious condition
than mere laziness. Directly opposed to joy, acedia denotes
a complex phenomenon whose symptoms include listlessness, torpor, moroseness, dejection, despair, depression, and
discouragement.

[23] Ibid., p. 197.

According to the early monastic writers, as exemplified by
Evagrius Ponticus (345–399), acedia is "a spiritual laziness,
an unhappiness with or aversion toward heavenly things, a
half-heartedness in spiritual warfare".[24] St. Thomas Aquinas,
who devotes an entire question to acedia in the *Summa Theologiae* (II–II, q. 35, aa. 1–4) and another in the *De Malo* (q. 11),
describes it as a sin against the joy born of charity, a joy that
arises from graced participation in the divine life. It is both a
sadness at the divine good (*tristitia de bono divino*), i.e., a sadness caused by the good of spiritual life that is life in union
with God, and an aversion to acting (*taedium operandi*).[25]

The English novelist and essayist Evelyn Waugh (1903–
1966) draws on this definition to emphasize that sloth is, in
the final analysis, a refusal of joy:

> What then is this Sloth which can merit the extremity of
> divine punishment? St. Thomas's answer is both comfort-
> ing and surprising: *tristitia de bono spirituali*, a sadness in the
> face of spiritual good. Man is made for joy in the love of
> God, a love which he expresses in service. If he deliber-
> ately turns away from that joy, he is denying the purpose of
> his existence. The malice of Sloth lies not merely in the
> neglect of duty (though that can be a symptom of it) but in
> the refusal of joy. It is allied to despair.[26]

Acedia hinders the dynamic of love in this life, which tends
toward union with God, and, since it is a sin against charity,
it likewise paralyses the gift of self and our openness toward

---

[24] Jean-Charles Nault, "Acedia: Enemy of Spiritual Joy", in *Communio*
(American ed.) 31 (2004): 237. For a detailed treatment of acedia, see Jean-
Charles Nault, *La Saveur de Dieu. L'acédie dans le dynamisme de l'agir* (Paris:
Cerf, 2006).

[25] For a discussion, see Nault, "Acedia", pp. 241–48.

[26] Evelyn Waugh, "Sloth", in *The Essays, Articles and Reviews of Evelyn Waugh*,
ed. Donat Gallagher (London: Methuen, 1983), p. 573.

the other. It so oppresses a man's spirit that he wants to do nothing.[27] Consequently, "it undoes the action of the Holy Spirit within human action, and it turns the human person away from his original orientation toward relationship with God and the joy which pours forth from it." [28] The man afflicted with acedia withdraws into himself; his action is no longer perceived as a gift of self but an uninhibited seeking of personal satisfaction in the fear of "losing" something.[29]

Joseph Ratzinger describes acedia as an "inertia of the heart", to be identified with the "sorrow of the world" that produces death (cf. 2 Cor 7:10).[30] It is rooted in a lack of hope and in a failure to attain genuine love. Since man's hunger is for the infinite, any hope or love that satisfies itself with something finite proves ultimately stale and disappointing.[31] The resulting sorrow stems from a lack of greatness of soul (*magnanimitas*), from an incapacity to believe in the lofty vocation to which God destines us. Ultimately, acedia or metaphysical inertia arises because man fails to accept that God is truly concerned about him, knows him, loves him, watches over him, and is close to him.[32] Instead, echoing the original temptation to be like God, he rebels against the greatness of having been chosen for life with God, for this makes too great a claim on him. However, in doing so, he rebels against his own nature, not wanting to be what he really is.

[27] See St. Thomas Aquinas, *Summa Theologiae*, II–II, q. 35, a. 1.

[28] Nault, "Acedia", p. 245.

[29] See ibid.

[30] See Ratzinger, *The Yes of Jesus Christ*, pp. 71–80. In his presentation, he draws on St. Thomas Aquinas, read through the lens of Josef Pieper; see Pieper, "On Hope", in his *Faith, Hope, Love* (San Francisco: Ignatius Press, 1997), pp. 87–138, especially pp. 117–23.

[31] See Ratzinger, *The Yes of Jesus Christ*, p. 73.

[32] See ibid., p. 74.

Acedia can affect society as well as individuals. Since the
greatness of the human vocation reaches beyond the individual aspect of human existence and cannot be contained
within the limits of the merely private, a society that turns
what is specifically human into something purely private and
defines itself in terms of complete secularity will of its nature
be sorrowful and a place of despair.[33] Far from being free, a
society that orders itself in accordance with an agnostic outlook has in fact surrendered to despair. Not being open to
the transcendent, it becomes dreary and boring, a gray world
without celebration, in which nothing else can happen because
man does no more than simply reproduce himself.[34] Even
the Church is not immune to the danger: "An excess of
external activity can be the pitiful attempt to cover up inward
pusillanimity and slothfulness of the heart that springs from
poverty of faith, from a lack of hope and of love for God
and for man made in his image and likeness." [35]

Along with despair, the slothful retreat before the greatness of humanity loved by God leads to what St. Thomas
calls *evagatio mentis*, the footloose restlessness of the mind,
which seeks to escape the deep-rooted sorrow that man cannot bear.[36] It reveals itself in loquaciousness, excessive curi-
osity, an irreverent urge "to pour oneself out from the peak
of the mind onto many things" (*importunitas*), interior restlessness and instability of place or purpose.[37] As Ratzinger

[33] See ibid., p. 76.

[34] See Joseph Ratzinger, *God Is Near Us: The Eucharist, the Heart of Life*
(San Francisco: Ignatius Press, 2003), p. 125.

[35] Ratzinger, *The Yes of Jesus Christ*, p. 77.

[36] See ibid.; also St. Thomas Aquinas, *De Malo*, q. 11, a. 4; Pieper, "On
Hope", pp. 120–21.

[37] St. Thomas Aquinas, *Summa Theologiae*, II–II, q. 35, a. 4 ad 3; see Pieper,
"On Hope", p. 121; Ratzinger, *The Yes of Jesus Christ*, p. 78.

points out, the diagnosis also indicates the appropriate med-
icine: "Only the courage to rediscover and accept the divine
dimension of our being can give our souls and our society a
new inner stability once again." [38]

St. Thomas also mentions four other "daughters of acedia": apathy or sluggish indifference (*torpor*) with regard to
what is needed for salvation; faintheartedness (*pusillanimi-
tas*) toward the mystical opportunities available to man; the
nursing of grudges (*rancor*) and spitefulness (*malitia*), which
is a conscious inner choice for evil as evil that has its source
in hatred for what is divine in man.[39]

Ratzinger devotes particular attention to rancor, which
is not to be confused with righteous indignation. It is man's
fundamental discontentedness with himself that, as it were,
takes its revenge on others because they do not provide
what could only be obtained by a new opening up of the
soul. Variants are to be observed not only in society but
also in the Church, where it stems ultimately from the fact
that people do not want from her what is her mission to
impart, the grace of being a child of God. Consequently,
they are bound to consider as inadequate everything else
that the Church is offering and are disappointed. The great
expectation of the Christian life is that it should bestow the
totally other, the ideal community, and with it the healing
of one's own inner self. This expectation is transferred to
the institutional and earthly aspect of the Church, which is
required to be the perfect community. Since in this life the
Church falls short of this ideal, an unholy rage results.[40]

---

[38] Ratzinger, *The Yes of Jesus Christ*, p. 78.

[39] See St. Thomas Aquinas, *De Malo*, q. 11, a. 4; *Summa Theologiae*, II–II,
q. 35, a. 4 ad 2; also St. Gregory the Great, *Moralia in Iob*, 31, 45, 88 (PL
76: 621).

[40] See Ratzinger, *The Yes of Jesus Christ*, pp. 78–79.

The failure lying at the root of the various manifestations of acedia is the refusal to acknowledge man's sublime vocation and engage in the spiritual combat. Acedia can be overcome only by accepting God's love and the greatness of our calling, which in turn give rise to Christian joy. At the beginning of his pontificate, Pope Benedict XVI indicated the remedy for the lack of spiritual joy characteristic of acedia and the fear accompanying it:

> Are we not perhaps all afraid in some way? If we let Christ enter fully into our lives, if we open ourselves totally to him, are we not afraid that he might take something away from us? Are we not perhaps afraid to give up something significant, something unique, something that makes life so beautiful? Do we not then risk ending up diminished and deprived of our freedom? ... No! If we let Christ into our lives, we lose nothing, nothing, absolutely nothing of what makes life free, beautiful and great. No! Only in this friendship are the doors of life opened wide. Only in this friendship is the great potential of human existence truly revealed. Only in this friendship do we experience beauty and liberation.[41]

Joyful perseverance in Christian living, which is made possible by allowing God's grace to bear fruit in a profound relationship of friendship with Christ, is the most effective defense against the assaults of the demons of acedia and the unmistakable criterion of an authentic spiritual life.[42]

3. Meaninglessness

Both boredom and acedia arise, as we have seen, from experiencing life as without purpose, aimless and, in the final

---

[41] Benedict XVI, Homily at the Mass for the inauguration of the Pontificate, April 24, 2005, in OR, April 27, 2005, p. 9.

[42] See Nault, "Acedia", p. 256.

analysis, meaningless. Nietzsche had rejected Christian morality because he saw it as an expression of the resentment felt
by those who envied the uninhibited actions of the strong
and, consequently, as a kind of "herd morality" inimical to
man's vital forces and his joy. However, immorality and lib-
ertinism also seem to enslave man, making him joyless and
empty. Given all this, must we conclude that man is an
absurd creature, as depicted in the theatre of Eugene Ionesco
or Samuel Beckett? Must we admit that his only hope is to
accept that there is no hope for him, that he is in reality
like Albert Camus' Sisyphus condemned to rolling his rock
uphill over and over again?[43]

For Joseph Ratzinger, it is not possible to accept that
man is absurd, since "we are so constructed that we must
find meaning if we are to live at all."[44] Meaning and joy
are closely connected: there can be true joy only if man
knows that his life has meaning, and such knowledge, in
turn, gives rise to inner harmony, joy, and peace.

Appealing to human experience, Ratzinger identifies as
the root of man's joy the harmony he enjoys with himself:
"Only the one who can accept himself can also accept the
thou, can accept the world."[45] However, it is not possible
to accept oneself by one's own efforts, for we "can love
ourselves only if we have first been loved by someone
else".[46] To live, not only do man's physical needs have to
be satisfied but also his basic longing to be appreciated

[43] See Ratzinger, "Faith as Trust and Joy", p. 78; Albert Camus, *Le Mythe de Sisyphe* (Paris: Gallimard, 1942). On the theatre of Beckett and Ionesco, see Martin Esslin, *The Theatre of the Absurd* (London: Eyre and Spottiswoode, 1962).

[44] Ratzinger, "Faith as Trust and Joy", p. 78.

[45] Ibid., p. 79.

[46] Ibid., p. 80.

and loved.[47] Elsewhere, Ratzinger says: "One cannot become *wholly* man in any other way than by being loved, by letting oneself be loved."[48]

Echoing the German philosopher Josef Pieper, whose writings were familiar to him from seminary days and with whom he became quite friendly during his years in Münster (1963–1966), Ratzinger explains that to love someone means to be able to say not simply with words but with one's whole being: "Yes, it is good that you exist."[49]

However, to be completely satisfactory, the love that gives me the courage to exist must be based on truth. It must be possible to answer affirmatively the question "Is it truly good that I exist?" Otherwise, the love that keeps me in existence will turn out to be no more than a tragic deception. Thus, so apparently simple an act as liking myself, of being at one with myself, actually raises the question of the whole universe. Love alone is of no avail: it needs truth

[47] Man thus needs both meaning and love in order to live; ultimately these are identical and rooted in the God of truth and love. As Ratzinger puts it: "Meaning is the bread on which man, in the intrinsically human part of his being, subsists. Without the word, without meaning, without love he falls into the situation of no longer being able to live, even when earthly comfort is present in abundance. . . . To believe as a Christian means in fact entrusting oneself to the meaning that upholds me and the world; taking it as the firm ground on which I can stand fearlessly" (*Introduction to Christianity*, 2nd ed. [San Francisco: Ignatius Press, 2004], p. 73).

[48] Ibid., p. 267.

[49] Ratzinger, "Faith as Trust and Joy", p. 80; see also his *The Yes of Jesus Christ*, pp. 89–91; Pieper, "On Love", in *Faith, Hope, Love*, p. 164. The original German edition of Pieper's work on love, *Über die Liebe*, was first published in 1972 and was to prove highly influential in the development of Ratzinger's thought. For an indication of Pieper's influence on Ratzinger, see Bernard N. Schumacher, "Philosophie de la culture: l'influence de Joseph Pieper dans la pensée de Joseph Ratzinger", in *Kephas* 17 (2006): 127–33.

on its side. "Only when love and truth are in harmony can man know joy." [50]

4. The Gospel of Joy

The Christian gospel answers the fundamental questions posed here. It proclaims the glad tidings that God is love and that he loves man. We therefore have reason to rejoice. Indeed, as Joseph Ratzinger emphasizes, the history of Christianity begins with the word "Rejoice!" [51] This was the greeting addressed to Mary by the angel Gabriel when he made known to her that she would be the mother of the long-awaited Savior (see Lk 1:28). While some exegetes, such as Raymond E. Brown, argue that the Greek imperative "*chaire*" used here is simply the usual form of greeting employed in the Hellenistic world, others, including Stanislas Lyonnet, René Laurentin, and Ignace de la Potterie, see a deeper meaning, an invitation to joy. [52] For them, as for Ratzinger, the evangelist, in using the term "*chaire*", is deliberately alluding to the messianic joy proclaimed in the Daughter of Zion oracles found in the prophets Zephaniah and Zechariah. [53]

[50] Ratzinger, "Faith as Trust and Joy", p. 80; cf. Joseph Ratzinger, "Vorfragen zu einer Theologie der Erlösung", in *Erlösung und Emanzipation*, ed. Leo Scheffczyk (Freiburg im Breisgau: Herder, 1973), pp. 141–55.

[51] See Ratzinger, "Faith as Trust and Joy", p. 75; Benedict XVI, Homily at the Mass for the Fourth Sunday of Advent, December 18, 2005, in OR, January 4, 2006, p. 11.

[52] See Raymond E. Brown, *The Birth of the Messiah*, rev. ed. (New York: Doubleday, 1993), pp. 319–24, 631; Stanislas Lyonnet, "*chaire, kecharitōmenē* (Réjouis-toi, comblée de grâce)", in *Biblica* 20 (1939): 131–41; René Laurentin, *Structure et théologie de Luc I–II* (Paris: Gabalda, 1957); Ignace de la Potterie, *Mary in the Mystery of the Covenant* (New York: Alba House, 1992), pp. 14–17.

[53] In the Septuagint, as de la Potterie points out (*Mary*, p. 14), the term "*chaire*" always appears in a context where Zion is invited to messianic joy

The figure of the Daughter of Zion is particularly significant for Joseph Ratzinger's Mariology and his teaching on joy. The expression "daughter of Zion" first makes its appearance in the prophet Micah (1:13), where it probably refers to a new suburb of Jerusalem, north of the Temple area, populated by poor, displaced exiles from the Northern Kingdom, who arrived after the fall of Samaria in 721 B.C.[54] To these, Micah addresses a message of encouragement and hope (see 4:8–13). Later, "daughter of Zion" comes to refer to Jerusalem as a whole (see Is 1:8; 10:32; 16:1) or to the city's population (see Is 37:22; 52:2; 62:11; Lam 4:22; Zeph 3:14; Zech 2:10; 9:9). It could easily be extended to Israel in her entirety (given the parallelism, this may be the case in Zeph 3:14). This figure is generally evoked in connection with the prophetic announcement of the mystery of election and covenant, the mystery of God's love for Israel. The Daughter of Zion is to rejoice, because God has cast out her enemies and is in her midst (see Zeph 3:14–15; Zech 2:10). She is to rejoice greatly and shout aloud, for her king comes to her, triumphant and victorious, "humble and riding on a donkey, on a colt the foal of a donkey" (Zech 9:9). In this way, the prophets encourage Israel to look forward in joyful expectation. Her joy is born of her trust in God that is solidly founded on his saving works in

---

as she looks to the future (see Joel 2:21–23; Zeph 3:14; Zech 9:9; cf. Lam 4:21). Mary is to rejoice in the eschatological joy promised to Zion and now accorded to her. On the Daughter of Zion, see Joseph Ratzinger, *Daughter Zion: Meditations on the Church's Marian Belief* (San Francisco: Ignatius Press, 1983), and his "Hail, Full of Grace: Elements of Marian Piety according to the Bible", in Hans Urs von Balthasar and Joseph Ratzinger, *Mary, the Church at the Source* (San Francisco: Ignatius Press, 2005), pp. 61–79.

[54] See Brown, *Birth*, p. 320.

the past, his consoling presence amid the trials of the present, and his promises regarding the future.

Israel's hope is fulfilled in the angel's announcement to Mary. As Ratzinger says, she is the Daughter of Zion: to her the Lord will come to take up his dwelling. She is the true Zion, toward whom all the long-held hopes of Israel are directed: indeed, she is the true Israel, in whom the old and new covenants, Israel and the Church, are inseparably one.[55] Hence, the Church learns what she is and what she is meant to be by looking to Mary, who is God's dwelling place, just as the Church must be.[56] Furthermore, she is the image of expectant mankind:

> As the true "daughter of Zion", Mary is the image of the Church, the image of believing man, who can come to salvation and to himself only through the gift of love—through grace.... She does not contest or endanger the exclusiveness of salvation through Christ; she points to it. She represents mankind, which as a whole is expectation and which needs this image all the more when it is in danger of giving up waiting and putting its trust in doing, which—indispensable as it is—can never fill the void that threatens man when he does not find that absolute love which gives him meaning, salvation, all that is truly necessary in order to live.[57]

[55] See Ratzinger, *Daughter Zion*, p. 43, and his *Introduction to Christianity*, 2nd ed., p. 272; on the indivisibility of Mary and the Church, see Second Vatican Council, Dogmatic Constitution on the Church, *Lumen Gentium*, November 21, 1964, chapter 8; also Hugo Rahner, *Our Lady and the Church* (Bethesda, Md.: Zaccheus Press, 2004).

[56] See Ratzinger, "Hail, Full of Grace", p. 66. Pope Benedict XVI developed similar ideas in the homily of the Mass celebrated on December 8, 2005, to mark the fortieth anniversary of the end of the Second Vatican Council; cf. OR, December 14, 2005, pp. 8–10.

[57] Ratzinger, *Introduction to Christianity*, 2nd ed., p. 280.

Mary's great hymn of joy, the Magnificat, which is inspired by numerous Old Testament passages, especially the song of Hannah (see 1 Sam 2:1–10), celebrates the goodness and mercy of God to individuals and to Israel as a whole, emphasizing that God comes to the help of the poor and simple, rather than to the proud and self-sufficient.[58]

The joy that pervades the entire New Testament is founded on the saving work that God carries out in our favor through the Incarnation, death, and Resurrection of his Son, Jesus Christ. Indeed, "God finds man so important that he himself has suffered for man." [59] The Cross is at the heart of the gospel, for it is the definitive approval of our existence; if God loves us to this point, then we are truly loved:

[58] There is a possibility that Luke discovered this hymn among the circles of the poor (*anawim*), where it was perhaps attributed to the Daughter of Zion, and he found it suitable to place it on the lips of Mary; see note *z* on Lk 1:46 in *The New Jerusalem Bible* (London: Darton, Longman and Todd, 1985), p. 1689. Denis McBride believes that the canticle, which is paralleled by psalms of the first and second centuries B.C., is Jewish rather than Christian in origin (see Denis McBride, *Emmaus: The Gracious Visit of God According to Luke* [Dublin: Dominican Publications, 1991], pp. 35–36). Joseph Fitzmyer argues to a pre-Lucan Jewish Christian source (see Joseph Fitzmyer, *The Gospel According to Luke I–IX* [New York: Doubleday, 1983], pp. 309–13). Raymond Brown holds that it may have originated among Jewish *anawim* who had converted to Christianity, but he makes no mention of a connection with the Daughter of Zion tradition (see Brown, *Birth*, pp. 350–55). The three major canticles of the Lucan infancy narrative are attributed to Mary, Zechariah, and Simeon, who are representative of the *anawim*, the poor of Yahweh. The *anawim*, with their characteristic spiritual attitude of lowliness, dependence on God, and Temple piety, lived in hopeful expectation of God's visit, which would bring the consolation promised to Israel (cf. Ps 149:4; Is 49:13; 66:2). On the connection of the Magnificat with *anawim* spirituality, see also Benedict XVI, General Audience, February 15, 2006, in OR, February 22, 2006, p. 11.

[59] Ratzinger, "Faith as Trust and Joy", p. 81.

Love is truth, and truth is love. Then life is worth living. This is the *evangelium*. This is why, even as the message of the Cross, it is glad tidings for one who believes; the only glad tidings that destroy the ambiguity of all other joys and make them worthy to be joy. Christianity is, by its very nature, joy—the ability to be joyful.[60]

Ratzinger asks how can Christian faith bestow on us today its power to liberate and make us joyful. The strength of the Christian message lies deeper than the events and activities that the Church organizes. The promise of love that makes life worthwhile remains firm, even when the messengers are themselves unprepossessing. That said, as he adds in a characteristic touch, it is no bad thing if a priest is entertaining, for deep joy of the heart is a true prerequisite for a sense of humor, and thus humor is, in a way, the measure of faith. The joy of the gospel reaches the roots of our existence and proves its strength not least in the fact that it sustains us when all about seems darkness.[61]

[60] Ibid.
[61] See ibid., pp. 81–82.

Chapter II

JOY AND TRUTH

At a time when the very existence of objective truth is strongly contested, Joseph Ratzinger has devoted considerable attention to the question of truth, without which genuine joy is impossible. The real problem of mankind, he maintains, is the darkening of truth; indeed, lack of truth is the major disease of our age.[1] This problem manifests itself at the personal, psychological level as an inability to be truthful and within culture and society in general as a denial of the existence of an objective binding truth accessible to all.

At the personal level, Ratzinger notes that inability to stand up for the truth and face the sometimes uncomfortable truth about ourselves hampers growth in personal maturity and freedom, leaving in its wake a dull sense of failure. At an interpersonal level, this inability generally results in group conformity that can quickly turn into a tyranny opposing

[1] See Joseph Ratzinger, "Preparation for Priestly Ministry", in *A New Song for the Lord: Faith in Christ and Liturgy* (New York: Crossroad, 1996), p. 213, and *Truth and Tolerance: Christian Belief and World Religions* (San Francisco: Ignatius Press, 2004), p. 66.

the truth. In such a situation, all our days turn gray and joy cannot thrive.[2]

Ratzinger devotes considerably more attention, however, to the problem of the denial of objective truth at the social and cultural level. He is convinced that by fidelity to God and to his revealed law, man "comes to experience himself as loved by God and discovers joy in truth and in righteousness—a joy in God which becomes his essential happiness".[3] Discovery of this joy is hindered today by the prevailing winds of relativism and a form of rationalism that is unwilling to consider the ultimate questions of life. At the Mass for the election of the Roman Pontiff on April 18, 2005, the then Cardinal Joseph Ratzinger warned of the dangers of relativism, which can affect even Christians, causing them to remain in the condition of children in the faith, "tossed back and forth and carried about with every wind of doctrine" (Eph 4:14). Relativism pervades much of modern thought, even at a popular level; indeed, he says, we are building "a dictatorship of relativism that does not recognize anything as definitive and whose ultimate goal consists solely of one's own ego and desires".[4]

On various occasions, Joseph Ratzinger has dealt with the problem of relativism, especially in his book *Truth and Tolerance*, which contains a collection of lectures and articles devoted to religious pluralism, faith, truth, tolerance, and freedom. In it, he identifies relativism, which espouses the view that there can be no objective truth, as "the most profound difficulty of our age", "in certain respects ... the real religion of modern

[2] See Ratzinger, *A New Song for the Lord*, pp. 212–15.

[3] Benedict XVI, Encyclical Letter *Deus Caritas Est*, December 25, 2005, no. 9 (Vatican City: Libreria Editrice Vaticana, 2006).

[4] Cardinal Joseph Ratzinger, Homily at the Mass for the election of the Roman Pontiff, April 18, 2005, in OR, April 20, 2005, p. 3.

man" and "the central problem for faith in our time".[5] Relativism can manifest itself in various ways, for example, in seeing all religions as of equal value and equally effective for salvation, thus dismissing Christianity's claim to possess the truth, or in denying the possibility of reaching objective knowledge about what cannot be empirically verified.[6]

Defining itself on the basis of the concepts of tolerance, dialectic epistemology, and freedom, "which would be limited by maintaining one truth as being valid for everyone", relativism is seen as the philosophical basis for democracy.[7] Democracy "is said to be founded on no one's being able to claim to know the right way forward; and it draws life from all the ways acknowledging each other as fragmentary attempts at improvement and trying to agree in common through dialogue".[8] Ratzinger agrees that in the realm of politics, the one single correct political option often does not exist. The construction of a freely ordered common life for men is something relative and cannot be absolute; thinking that it could be was the error of Marxism and the political theologies. While one cannot deny relativism a certain right in the political realm, Ratzinger cautions against absolute relativism: some things, such as killing innocent people, are always wrong and can never become right, just as other things are right and can never become wrong.[9]

[5] Ratzinger, *Truth and Tolerance*, pp. 72, 84, 117.

[6] For a discussion of religious pluralism, with particular reference to the philosophical and theological presuppositions underlying pluralist theologies of religion, see Cardinal Joseph Ratzinger's presentation (September 5, 2000) of the Declaration *Dominus Iesus* in his *Pilgrim Fellowship of Faith: The Church as Communion* (San Francisco: Ignatius Press, 2005), pp. 209–16.

[7] Ratzinger, *Truth and Tolerance*, p. 117.

[8] Ibid.

[9] See ibid., pp. 117–18. For Ratzinger's views on the relationship of religion, politics, and ethics, see the lecture which he delivered in response to

However, relativism, which entails the renunciation of the claim to know the truth, cannot provide the ultimate foundation for democracy. Far from protecting the freedom that democracy extols, the abandonment of truth would eventually lead to a dictatorship of tolerance and the manipulation of freedom itself, as the history of the twentieth century so frighteningly demonstrates. To survive and flourish, a democratic culture requires foundational values, which include respect for the dignity of all human life, the recognition and safeguarding of human rights, particularly the right to religious freedom, and the willingness to be guided by fundamental moral principles and objective truths.[10]

Further problems arise when relativism is applied in the areas of religion and ethics. Ratzinger refers to John Hick's relativist theory of religion, which rejects the identity of the historical figure of Jesus Christ with the living God as a relapse into myth, and Paul F. Knitter's attempt to combine a pluralist theology of religions with liberation theologies in such a way as to stress the priority of orthopraxy over orthodoxy.[11] The relativism of the positions of Hick

---

Jürgen Habermas at the Bavarian Catholic Academy on January 19, 2004: "That Which Holds the World Together: The Pre-political Moral Foundation of a Free State", in Jürgen Habermas and Joseph Ratzinger, *The Dialectics of Secularization: On Reason and Religion* (San Francisco: Ignatius Press, 2006), pp. 53–80; see also D. Vincent Twomey, "Zur Theologie des Politischen", in Joseph Ratzinger et al., *Vom Wiederauffinden der Mitte, Grundorientierung: Texte aus vier Jahrzehnten* (Freiburg im Breisgan: Herder, 1997), pp. 219–30.

[10] For a brief discussion of Ratzinger's teaching on the necessity of respect for the truth in cultural and political life, see Serge-Thomas Bonino, "Coopérateurs de la vérité: Joseph Ratzinger et la vérité", in *Kephas* 17 (2006): 79–88.

[11] See Ratzinger, *Truth and Tolerance*, pp. 119–26; John Hick, *Evil and the God of Love* (London: Macmillan, 1966); John Hick, *An Interpretation of Religion: Human Responses to the Transcendent* (New Haven: Yale University Press, 1989); Paul F. Knitter, *No Other Name? A Critical Survey of Christian Attitudes toward the World Religions* (Maryknoll, N.Y.: Orbis Books, 1985).

and Knitter and of other related theories is ultimately based
on a rationalism that holds that reason in the sense given to
it by Immanuel Kant (1724–1804) is incapable of any metaphysical knowledge.[12] Consequently, religion is presented
in pragmatic terms, as an ethical or political program.

In contrast to the rationalist approaches of Hick and Knitter, there also exists a consciously antirationalist response to
the notion that all is relative, namely, the complex reality of
"New Age", whose practitioners seek to overcome subjective consciousness "in a re-entry into the dance of the cosmos through ecstasy".[13] According to this form of modern
"mysticism", God is not a personal reality, distinct from the
world, but the spiritual energy at work throughout the universe. In simple terms, for the various forms of New Age,
religion means bringing oneself into tune with the cosmic
whole, the transcending of all divisions. In order to be free,
man must let himself be dissolved.

Closely connected with the various forms of relativism
in denying that we can know ultimate truth is a kind of
rationalism that limits the capacities of reason to what can
be known by the methods of the natural sciences.[14] The
laws of scientific method, which brought it success when

[12] See Ratzinger, *Truth and Tolerance*, p. 126. Hick makes use of the Kant-
ian distinction between phenomenon and noumenon: we can never know
ultimate reality in itself, but only its appearances in the way we perceive
things. Similarly, Knitter appeals to Kant for his denial that the absolute can
exist in history.

[13] Ibid., p. 127.

[14] On the progressive abandonment of the Scholastic equating of being
and truth (*verum est ens*), the development of the historical approach to the
question of truth (*verum quia factum*) and the turn toward technical thinking
(*verum quia faciendum*), and the consequences of all this for understanding the
nature of Christianity and belief, see Joseph Ratzinger, *Introduction to Christianity*, 2nd ed. (San Francisco: Ignatius Press, 2004), pp. 57–69.

applied to the physical world, have, through their general-
ization, paradoxically become its prison. Reason has tended
to limit itself to what can be verified or experienced. Such
an approach is necessary and correct within the specific path
followed by natural science, but if it is declared the absolute and unsurpassable form of human thought, then man
is rendered incapable of answering the most essential questions of life, about where he comes from and where he is
going, and what he may or may not do. It must be borne
in mind that "knowledge of the functional aspect of the
world, as procured for us so splendidly by present-day technical and scientific thinking, brings with it no understanding of the world and of being." [15] For this to occur, and to
overcome the danger of man's "forgetting to reflect on himself and on the meaning of his existence",[16] rationality must
open itself once again to the ultimate questions, employing
varying methods depending on the nature of its object: imma-
terial things "cannot be approached with methods appropriate to what is material".[17] Man dishonors reason by
abandoning the most important questions of life to feeling,
which can never give a satisfactory response.[18]

An atrophied rationalism of this kind does serious damage in the realm of faith. Christianity's claim to be true
cannot be verified by scientific methods, "because the kind
of experiment demanded—pledging one's life for this—is
of a quite different kind".[19] While the saints, who have
undergone this experiment, can stand as guarantors of
the truth of Christianity, this evidence can be disregarded

[15] Ibid., p. 77.
[16] Ibid., p. 71.
[17] Ratzinger, *Truth and Tolerance*, p. 194.
[18] See ibid., pp. 156–58.
[19] Ibid., p. 226.

and frequently is. Many practitioners of biblical exegesis, operating on philosophical preconceptions similar to those of Hick and Knitter, have fallen victim to narrow forms of rationalism. By excluding what does not come under the purview of scientific method, they end up denying the reality of miracles, the divinity of Christ, and the very possibility of divine intervention in the world.[20] Furthermore, skepticism about the possibility of knowing ultimate truth leads to a "gray pragmatism" in the everyday life of the Church, "whereby everything is apparently being done right, yet in reality the faith is stale and declining into a shabby meanness".[21] Symptoms of this are attempts to decide questions of faith and morals by majority votes and the notion that the liturgy is ultimately a self-expression of the local community, subject to its creative whims. However, a faith decided by ourselves is no faith at all.[22]

The relativist and rationalist denial of man's capacity to know ultimate truth, in the final analysis, fails to satisfy. Man is made for truth; in this lies his innate dignity.[23] He cannot avoid posing the ultimate questions regarding his origin and destiny, regarding life and death. Indeed, in all cultures we find attempts to answer these questions. Christianity has more in common with these cultures than with "the relativistic and rationalistic world that has cut loose from the fundamental insights of mankind and is thus leading man into a vacuum, devoid of meaning, which risks being fatal for him

---

[20] See ibid., pp. 130–36, 186. Christianity, however, emphasizes God's making himself definitively known in the unique historical figure of Jesus Christ; see Ratzinger, *Pilgrim Fellowship of Faith*, p. 210.

[21] Ratzinger, *Truth and Tolerance*, p. 129.

[22] See ibid., pp. 129–30.

[23] See ibid., p. 191.

unless the answer to it comes to him in time".[24] Ratzinger
continues:

> For the knowledge that man must turn toward God and
> toward what is eternal, is found right across all cultures; the
> knowledge about sin, repentance, and forgiveness; the knowl-
> edge concerning communion with God and eternal life;
> and finally the knowledge of the basic rules of morality, as
> they are found in the form of the Ten Commandments. It
> is not relativism that is confirmed; rather, it is the unity of
> the human condition and its common experience of con-
> tact with a truth that is greater than we are.[25]

Ratzinger observes that cultures are, on the one hand,
differentiated one from another, and, on the other, as dynamic
realities, they are open to one another and are capable of
mutually purifying one another and of merging with one
another. He attributes the agreement in essentials found in
cultures far removed from one another to the fact that man
is a single being, one and the same, who is "touched and
affected in the very depth of his existence by truth itself",
by the truth spoken by God himself.[26] The variety, which
can in some cases lead to a closed attitude, comes in the
first instance from the limitations of the human mind, for
no one can grasp the whole of anything. Rather, many and
varied perceptions and forms come together in a sort of
mosaic: in order to form the whole, each one needs all the
others. This, of course, is too optimistic a picture: the poten-
tial universality of cultures is often blocked by various insur-
mountable obstacles that prevent it from turning into an
actual universality. While man is secretly touched by the

[24] Ibid., p. 79.
[25] Ibid.
[26] Ibid., p. 65; for a description of the nature of culture, see ibid., pp. 193–97.

truth spoken by God, there is also an opposing negative
factor in human existence that, at least partially, cuts people
off from the truth and from one another. This undeniable
negative factor of alienation causes the real difficulty for
the struggle to bring about any meeting of cultures. Given
these positive and negative facts, one can neither reject the
world's religions as reprehensible superstitions nor give a
solely positive evaluation of them.[27]

The real problem of mankind is the "darkening of truth",
which distorts our actions and sets us against one another,
"because we bear our own evil within ourselves, are alienated from ourselves, cut off from the ground of our being,
from God".[28] The greater and purer a given culture is, the
more man's inner openness to God is influential in it, and
the more prepared it is for the revelation of God, which is
not something alien to it but corresponds to an inner expectation of the culture itself.[29] If truth is offered, this means
a leading out of alienation; "it means the vision of a common standard that does no violence to any culture but that
guides each one to its own heart, because each exists ultimately as an expectation of truth." [30] This does not produce uniformity, but complementarity, for every culture can
develop and be fruitful in its own way in relation to the
common standard.

In the face of general skepticism regarding any claim to
truth as far as religions are concerned, the Christian faith

[27] See ibid., pp. 19, 65; also Ratzinger, *Pilgrim Fellowship of Faith*, pp. 213–15.

[28] Ratzinger, *Truth and Tolerance*, p. 66.

[29] See ibid., p. 195. Pope John Paul II develops this point in the encyclical
Fides et Ratio, September 15, 1998, nos. 70–72, making special reference to
the encounter between Christian faith, shaped in the Graeco-Roman world,
and the cultures of India.

[30] Ratzinger, *Truth and Tolerance*, p. 67.

puts forward a unique truth claim, transcending all cultural
particularities, since it professes to know and proclaim the
one true God and the Savior of all mankind: "There is salvation in no one else, for there is no other name under
heaven given among men by which we must be saved" (Acts
4:12).[31] Christianity teaches us that the ultimate value is
not the unnamable but "that mysterious unity created by
love and which is represented, beyond all our categories, in
the Trinity and unity of God, which for its part is the highest picture of the reconciliation of unity and multiplici-
ty".[32] The last word about being is not the unnamable or
unknowable absolute, but love, which makes itself visible in
Jesus Christ, the God who becomes a creature and unites
the creature with the Creator. Essentially, Christian salvation involves a relationship with God, based on love, that
becomes a union in accordance with the Pauline principle
that God will be "all in all" (see 1 Cor 15:28), without
suppressing the distinction between "I" and "Thou".[33]

While there is a good deal that needs purifying and opening up in the particular cultural forms in which it manifests
itself, Christianity is certain that "it is at heart the self-
revelation of truth itself and, therefore, redemption." [34] It
proclaims Jesus Christ, the truth in person and, thereby, the
way to be human.[35] Scripture teaches that man is capable
of the truth and able to recognize it. Man can indeed know
the fundamental truths about himself, about his origin and
future: Christian faith "furnishes him with a knowledge
which alone makes sense of everything else which he

[31] See ibid., pp. 9, 19.
[32] Ibid., p. 84.
[33] See ibid., p. 45.
[34] Ibid., p. 66.
[35] See ibid., p. 67.

knows".[36] The Bible confronts man with the truth that has made itself known as a person in Jesus Christ.[37] Jesus' words "I am the way, and the truth, and the life" (Jn 14:6) express the basic claim of the Christian faith: "It is the peculiarity of Christianity, in the realm of religions, that it claims to tell us the truth about God, the world, and man and lays claim to being the *religio vera*, the religion of truth." [38] Were it to renounce its claim to truth, faith itself would be reduced to a subjective consolation, to make-believe. Such a faith, however, does not help us in living and dying and, in any case, would fail to satisfy for long, since man is not content to remain in the dark where essential questions are concerned.[39]

When the Christian message encountered the religions and great currents of thought of the ancient world, it found its point of contact not with the mythical images and vague notions behind the pagan religions but with the philosophical enlightenment that sought to discover the truth about the divine presence and the foundations of the world.[40] What this means is that Christian faith is not based on poetry or politics, the two great sources of religion, but on knowledge, which leads to worship of the true God. Since Christianity involved a process of demythologizing and the victory

[36] Joseph Ratzinger, *The Nature and Mission of Theology: Approaches to Understanding Its Role in the Light of Present Controversy* (San Francisco: Ignatius Press, 1995), p. 92.

[37] See Ratzinger, *Truth and Tolerance*, p. 95.

[38] Ibid., p. 184.

[39] See ibid., pp. 162–65, 216–17; also Ratzinger, *The Nature and Mission of Theology*, p. 92.

[40] On this point, see the discussion on St. Augustine's use of Marcus Terentius Varro's distinction between the three kinds of theology found in the ancient world (mythical, civic, natural) in Ratzinger's doctoral thesis *Volk und Haus Gottes*, chapter 9, § 21, and in *Truth and Tolerance*, pp. 165–70. For a more general treatment of this issue, see Ratzinger, *Introduction to Christianity*, 2nd ed., pp. 137–50.

of knowledge and truth, it could not be considered as a specific religion seeking to establish itself in place of others, but simply as the truth that renders mere appearance superfluous. Because Christianity refused to accept the relativism and interchangeability of the images found in the various pagan religions, thus obstructing the political purpose of these religions, it was considered both "atheistic" and subversive.[41]

Christianity did not simply identify the true God with the God of the philosophers, understood as pure being or pure thought, whose eternity and unchangeable nature preclude any relation with what is changing and transitory.[42] Philosophical thought underwent a profound transformation in its encounter with Christianity. While the philosophical God is essentially self-centered, the God of faith is one who speaks to man and to whom one can pray. The Christian God is not a remote "supreme being" but concerns himself with man. While the God of the philosophers is pure thought, the God of faith, as thought, is agape, the power of creative love: "This thought is creative because, as thought, it is love, and, as love, it is thought."[43] From this, it is clear that truth and love, when completely realized, as they are in God, are identical.[44]

---

[41] See Ratzinger, *Truth and Tolerance*, p. 170, and his *Introduction to Christianity*, 2nd ed., pp. 142–43. In the late classical world, Christians were called "atheists" not because they denied the existence of God but because they challenged the validity of the pagan religious system, which was regarded as essential to the well-being and security of the State. Hence, they were considered a threat to the established social order; on this, see Alister McGrath, *The Twilight of Atheism: The Rise and Fall of Disbelief in the Modern World* (New York: Doubleday, 2004), pp. 8–9.

[42] See Ratzinger, *Introduction to Christianity*, 2nd ed., pp. 143–48.

[43] Ibid., p. 148.

[44] In another context, Ratzinger expresses it in this way: "Full truth is part of full love"; see Joseph Ratzinger, *Theological Highlights of Vatican II*

While the paganism of the ancient world failed to satisfy, Christianity proved successful because it corresponded both to the demands of reason and to man's religious needs, and because it provided a serious morality, a path of living, based on the commandment to love God and neighbor. The God proclaimed by the Christian faith, the God of truth and love, is both the God whose existence can be established by reason and the God who has entered history, revealing himself in Jesus Christ.[45] For Christianity, nature, God, man, ethics, and religion are indissolubly linked together: this interlinking contributed to make it appear "the obvious choice in the crisis concerning the gods and in the crisis concerning the enlightenment of the ancient world".[46] Ratzinger continues:

> The orientation of religion toward a rational view of reality as a whole, ethics as part of this vision, and its concrete application under the primacy of love became closely associated. The primacy of the Logos and the primacy of love proved to be identical. The Logos was seen to be, not merely a mathematical reason at the basis of all things, but a creative love taken to the point of becoming sympathy, suffering with the creature. The cosmic aspect of religion, which reverences the Creator in the power of being, and its existential aspect, the question of redemption, merged together and became one.[47]

(New York: Paulist Press, 1966), p. 24. (I am grateful to Fr. John M. Cunningham, O.P., for this reference.)

[45] See Ratzinger, *Truth and Tolerance*, pp. 170–75.

[46] Ibid., p. 182. Referring to the perspective adopted by the *Catechism of the Catholic Church*, Ratzinger affirms that "the question of man and the question of God are inextricably woven together" (Joseph Ratzinger, *Gospel, Catechesis, Catechism: Sidelights on the Catechism of the Catholic Church* [San Francisco: Ignatius Press, 1997], p. 15).

[47] Ratzinger, *Truth and Tolerance*, p. 182.

The faith of Israel showed the harmony between God and the world, between reason and mystery, as well as giving moral guidance. While there was an incipient universalism in Israel's faith, a non-Jew could only ever stand in the outer circle of this religion. Christianity brought about the decisive breakthrough; having "broken down the dividing wall" (Eph 2:14), it enabled everyone to belong to the one God. The new Christian synthesis is well expressed in a confession in the First Letter of St. John: "We know and believe the love" (4:16). Through Christ we have discovered creative love: the rational principle of the universe has revealed itself as love.[48] Elsewhere, Ratzinger puts it in these terms:

> Christian faith lives on the discovery that not only is there such a thing as objective meaning but that this meaning knows me and loves me, that I can entrust myself to it like the child who knows that everything he may be wondering about is safe in the "you" of his mother.[49]

All of this indicates that if Christianity is to recover its persuasive force in the midst of the present crisis for mankind, it must show itself once again as the religion of truth and the religion of love. It must be based on both orthodoxy and orthopraxy: "At the most profound level its content will necessarily consist . . . in love and reason coming together as the two pillars of reality: the true reason is love and love is the true reason. They are in their unity the true basis and the goal of all reality." [50]

Christian faith, not the watered-down version proposed by the relativists or by those who reduce it to a question of

[48] See ibid., pp. 154–56.
[49] Ratzinger, *Introduction to Christianity*, 2nd ed., p. 80.
[50] Ratzinger, *Truth and Tolerance*, p. 183.

feeling or personal opinion divorced from truth, but the
"full and joyful faith of the New Testament, of the Church
down the ages", continues to have a chance in the contemporary world.[51] It does so because it corresponds to the
nature of man, who has an unquenchable thirst for the infinite, for truth and for love. Christian mission, far from being
a form of cultural imperialism, is a matter of spreading the
liberating truth and love that everyone needs.[52] Truth is a
gift for everyone and alienates no one. In Christ, the essential gift of truth is offered to everyone, and it is our duty to
share this gift freely with others.

Christian faith understood in this full sense leads to joy.
Joy is grounded in both love and truth. As a gift received,
it depends on God's love—revealed to us by the Son, who
makes the Father known to us—and is poured into our hearts
by the Holy Spirit—the embrace of love between the Father
and the Son, and the Paraclete who leads us into the fullness of truth. Our joy flows from allowing God's gifts to
bear fruit in us: it arises from our response of love to God's
love, according to the commandment to love God and neighbor, and from our readiness to face the truth about ourselves and defend the objective truth about God and man.
This joy, since it comes from God, is unfailing: despite the
trials of this life and ever more vocal opposition to the truth,
it cannot be overcome.

Joseph Ratzinger's reflections on the grounding of
joy in God and on the link between joy and truth owe
much not only to Scripture but also, in all likelihood, to
St. Augustine. In his *Confessions*, the Bishop of Hippo
employs the famous expression *gaudium de veritate* to stress

[51] Ibid., p. 137.
[52] See ibid., pp. 56, 73, and Ratzinger, *Pilgrim Fellowship of Faith*, p. 215.

the connection between truth and joy (see 10, 23, 33).
Augustine came late to knowledge of true joy (see 2, 2, 2),
after learning by bitter experience that while all seek joy
and happiness, some searching here, some there, it is illu-
sory to think that any kind of joy whatsoever will produce
happiness (see 10, 21, 31–22, 32). The wicked man cannot
experience true joy, for his joy is always contaminated by
the bitterness of remorse and the fear of divine or human
retribution. Placing his joy in material things, he does not
know the higher joys of the spirit. That said, in pursuing
another joy and not the true one, the will remains drawn
toward some image of the true joy. There are various kinds
of joy, which are pale images of true joy, for example, the
joy experienced when something lost is found, the joy
acquired only at the cost of suffering, the joy of a positive
response to repeated prayer, and the joy of friendship (see
8, 3, 7–8; 12, 30). Joy has an interpersonal dimension for it
is increased by being shared (see 8, 4, 9; 10, 4, 6). However, joy is insecure if it is not rooted in God (see 6, 6, 10),
because true joy (see 7, 7, 11), the only joy possible (see
10, 23, 33), comes from God (see 8, 11, 27; 10, 22, 32) and
is founded on the truth that is God (see 10, 23, 33–34; 36,
59). Augustine is convinced that happiness is to be found
only in pursuing true joy, which is in God alone: "That is
the authentic happy life, to set one's joy on you, grounded
in you and caused by you.... The happy life is joy based
on the truth. This is joy grounded in you, O God, who are
the truth." [53] God is the supreme Good who alone can satisfy man's deepest needs and desires, thus making him

---

[53] St. Augustine, *Confessions*, 10,22,32–23,33: "Et ipsa est beata vita, gau-
dere ad te, de te, propter te ... Beata quippe vita est gaudium de veritate.
Hoc est enim gaudium de te, qui veritas est, Deus". I have followed Henry
Chadwick's translation of the *Confessions*, published by Oxford University

supremely happy; any other good can only give a partial
and limited happiness.

Augustine now reflects on a dilemma (see 10, 23, 33–34).
People generally say that they want to be happy and desire
true joy. They love the truth because they do not wish to
be deceived, and when they love the happy life, they are
unquestionably loving the truth. They somehow know that
there is a connection between truth and the happy life, which
means there must be some knowledge of truth in their memory. Yet, many do not find their joy in this; they are unhappy.
Augustine ascribes their unhappiness to the fact that they
are more occupied with other things that make them more
wretched than with the truth that would make them happy
and about which they remember so little. There is a rupture between their knowing the truth and loving it; this
rupture is the continuous torment that afflicts sinners. Their
love for the truth takes the form of loving something else
that they want to be the truth. For the sake of what it is
they love instead of the truth, they hate truth itself. Since
they do not wish to be deceived, they are unwilling to be
told they are mistaken and so they do not listen to the mes-
senger of the truth (cf. Gal 4:16). They love the truth when
it reveals itself but hate it when it reveals them. However,
truth denied will repay those who deny it: those who were
unwilling to be discovered by the truth will be unmasked
by it against their wills, but to them truth will not make
itself known.

Yet, even in its miserable condition, the human mind
prefers to find joy in true rather than in false things. It will
be happy if it comes to find joy only in that truth by which

Press in 1991. For the references cited in this paragraph, see S. Agostino, *Le
Confessioni*, ed. Giuliano Vigini (Cinisello Balsamo: San Paolo, 2001), p. 482.

all things are true. From this, it is clear that true joy can only arise from a right ordering of one's affections and desires, which involves not only knowing but also loving the truth, God, above all things.

St. Augustine's insistence on the inseparability of joy and truth, so well expressed in the memorable formula "*gaudium de veritate*", finds a powerful echo in the writings of Joseph Ratzinger. Like the Doctor of Grace, Ratzinger knows that true joy can be found only in knowing and loving the God of truth, who alone satisfies the human longing for meaning and enduring happiness.[54] Far from being a burden, the truth that is discovered in encounter with the One who alone is Truth leads to authentic and unfailing joy.

[54] See Joseph Ratzinger, *Jesus of Nazareth: From the Baptism in the Jordan to the Transfiguration* (New York: Doubleday, 2007), 353–54.

Chapter III

LIVING JOY IN FAITH, HOPE, AND LOVE

Shortly before his death, the German exegete Heinrich Schlier, often cited by Joseph Ratzinger, affirmed that "to be Christian means joy".[1] This joy is inseparable from the Cross, but it is also a joy that only God, not the world, can give. Christian joy accompanies a life lived in response to God's love and is ultimately due to our sharing in the life of the Blessed Trinity, which is brought about by Christ's saving work and the indwelling of the Holy Spirit.

1. Faith

Joy is inseparable from the basic supernatural attitudes of faith, hope, and love, traditionally called the theological virtues. Faith is the fundamental act of Christian existence, which expresses the essential structure of Christianity and indicates how we are to live in order to reach the ultimate goal of human life.[2]

---

[1] See Hans Urs von Balthasar, "Premessa", in Heinrich Schlier, *La lettera ai Filippesi*, trans. Bruno Ognibeni (Milan: Jaca Book, 1993), p. 7.

[2] See Joseph Ratzinger, *Christianity and the Crisis of Cultures* (San Francisco: Ignatius Press, 2006), p. 77, and his *The Yes of Jesus Christ: Spiritual*

In a 1989 lecture entitled "What Does It Mean to Believe?" Ratzinger considers the attitudes necessary for a correct approach to the question of God.[3] Agnosticism, though initially appealing because of its lack of dogmatic commitment and its recognition of the limits of human scientific knowing, is no solution to the God-question. The thirst for the infinite is an essential dimension of human nature. We cannot simply put aside the fundamental questions (Where do I come from? Where am I going? What is the measure of my being?) as though they did not impinge on everyday life. The question of God is, in fact, eminently practical, because it affects all spheres of life. While one could accept agnosticism as a theoretical position, in practice we must decide between one of two possibilities: to live as though God exists or to live as though he does not. Hence, the question of God is not a neutral one, for the way we live our lives depends on our answer to it.[4]

Our true vocation is to the truth, but, as St. Paul shows in the first chapter of the Letter to the Romans, there are many obstacles to responding to it, above all our own pride, self-sufficiency, and desire to dominate reality, turning it into nothing more than our servant. History shows that there

---

Exercises in Faith, Hope and Love (New York: Crossroad, 2005), p. 4. Ratzinger provides a more complete account of the nature of Christian faith in *Introduction to Christianity*, 2nd ed. (San Francisco: Ignatius Press, 2004), pp. 39–100, and in various articles in *Principles of Catholic Theology* (San Francisco: Ignatius Press, 1987). On this theme, see Luc-Thomas Somme, "Une réflexion fondamentale sur la foi", in *Kephas* 17 (2006): 23–33.

[3] This lecture, delivered on March 11, 1989, at the *Scuola di Cultura Cattolica* in Bassano del Grappa, is contained in Ratzinger, *Christianity and the Crisis of Cultures*, pp. 75–116. Ratzinger develops similar ideas in the first chapter of *The Yes of Jesus Christ*.

[4] See Ratzinger, *Christianity and the Crisis of Cultures*, pp. 87–89, and his *The Yes of Jesus Christ*, pp. 11–13.

is a constant tension between, on the one hand, the non-
violent, tranquil claims made by the truth, and, on the other,
the pressure to make profit and the need to have a good
relationship with the powers that determine daily life.[5] As
Ratzinger insists, the majesty of truth reveals itself only to
the watchful and humble heart; in order to hear it, we must
be prepared to take the risk of assuming the attitude of
humble listeners.[6] The correct approach to answering the
question of God demands certain qualities: alertness to the
deeper dimensions of reality, readiness to ask about the totality of our human existence and reality in general, humility
before the greatness of truth, willingness to be purified by
and for the truth, readiness to listen to the great witnesses
of God, purity of heart, and commitment of time and energy
to this question, which personally affects each one of us.[7]
If we hearken to the voice of our essential nature, to the
voice of creation, and let ourselves be led by this, we can
come to know God. This principle, laid down by St. Paul,
is still valid today, but we need God's help: we need him to
cross the threshold and speak to us, if we are to enter into
a real relationship with him.

The ecclesial dimension of faith re-emerges in this context.[8] God's speaking to us reaches us though those who
have listened to him and come into contact with him. Our
relationship with God is inseparable from our relationship
with others. In supernatural faith, the many depend on the

[5] See Ratzinger, *Christianity and the Crisis of Cultures*, p. 98.

[6] See ibid., p. 99.

[7] See ibid., pp. 90–91, and Ratzinger, *The Yes of Jesus Christ*, pp. 19–21.

[8] For a more developed version of what is briefly sketched in *Christianity and the Crisis of Cultures* and in *The Yes of Jesus Christ* regarding the ecclesial form of faith, see *Introduction to Christianity*, 2nd ed., pp. 82–100, and *Principles of Catholic Theology*, especially pp. 15–190.

few who have firsthand experience of God, and the few live for the many. Jesus Christ is the revelation of the Father: "He who has seen me has seen the Father" (Jn 14:9). Christian faith is essentially a sharing in what Jesus sees: his act of seeing is mediated by his word, which is the authentic expression of what he sees.[9] Our faith depends also on the experience of the saints, in whom the light of Christ shines in a particularly intense way. While we are, at first, believers "at second hand", dependent on what others have seen, we gradually grow in faith through our own experiences. Christ's message answers an inner expectation of our heart: it corresponds to an inner light of our being that reaches out toward the truth of God.[10] Gradually, despite possible setbacks on the way, we come to see more clearly for ourselves what we believed, just as the Samaritan woman's neighbors did, having initially believed on the strength of her testimony (see Jn 4:42). Christians today have a great responsibility in a world that no longer knows God: their faith and their witness to the truth should serve as a point of reference for those who seek God, especially in the darkness of a world that is largely opposed to God.[11]

Faith, although it is a personal act, does not occur in isolation. It involves communion with Christ and unity with all those who have followed him. In accordance with the insight expressed in St. Paul's words "it is no longer I who live, but Christ who lives in me" (Gal 2:20), Christian faith involves shattering the isolation of my own "I" in order to rediscover myself and come to maturity in the larger "I" of the body of Christ. Hence, faith is a personal act that is

[9] See Ratzinger, *Christianity and the Crisis of Cultures*, pp. 104–105, and his *The Yes of Jesus Christ*, p. 29.

[10] See Ratzinger, *Christianity and the Crisis of Cultures*, p. 110.

[11] See ibid., p. 112.

ecclesial in character: it lives and moves in the "we" of the
Church, since it makes us one with the "I" of Christ.[12] It
is clear from all of this that I cannot build my own personal
faith in an isolated dialogue with Christ. If faith does not
live in the "we" of the Church, it does not live at all. The
"I" cannot be separated from the "we", just as faith, truth,
and life cannot be separated. The Church, then, is the place
where we encounter the true God, revealed to us by the
Son: only by journeying with others along the path of faith
do we advance toward the God whose call to a relationship
with him is present in every human heart.

2. Hope

Christian hope presupposes faith.[13] Hope is to be carefully
distinguished from naïve optimism, which could simply be a
denial of reality, and from ideological optimism, exemplified
on the one hand by the liberal faith in progress through evolution and the scientifically guided development of human
history, and on the other by the Marxist faith in the dialec-
tical movement of history, which progresses by means of
the class struggle and revolution. While the goal of such kinds
of optimism is the utopian perfect society, achieved through
human effort, that of Christian hope is the Kingdom of
God. The justification of Christian hope is the Incarnation
of God's Word and love in Jesus Christ. God has already
manifested his love in history and has begun his age in Christ.
In contrast, the various forms of ideological optimism fail to

---

[12] See ibid., p. 114.

[13] On hope, see Ratzinger, *The Yes of Jesus Christ*, pp. 39–68, Joseph Rat-
zinger, "On Hope", in *Communio* (American edition) 12 (1985): 71–84;
Benedict XVI, Encyclical Letter *Spe Salvi*, November 30, 2007 (Vatican City:
Libreria Editrice Vaticana, 2007).

answer the deepest questions about human existence and are utterly incapable of facing the problem of death, which they avoid with various subterfuges.

Hope, because it is built on faith and truth, is not blindly optimistic and it rejects unreasonable expectations, relying instead on God's promises. In Scripture, this attitude is exemplified by the prophet Jeremiah's rejection of the official mendacious optimism in the face of the Babylonian threat and his proclamation of realism coupled with a stirring message of hope (see Jer 28–31). Similarly, the Book of Revelation presents a vision of history that is antithetical to blind faith in perpetual progress and the possibility of establishing a perfect society by merely human activity. However, the last book of the Bible does preach a message of hope. God will not allow human history to be torn from his hands: his power is stronger than all the frightfulness of our world, and the last word is not one of death but of love.

Hope is centered on Christ, who invites us to build our house on solid foundations, the rock that his word is (see Mt 7:24–27). More precisely, he invites us to allow him to build the house (see Mt 16:13–20). By our own strength alone, it is not possible for us to construct our lives on a completely solid base. We must not build in isolation but with Christ, who in the Sermon on the Mount (Mt 5–7) teaches us what it means to be Christian. The Sermon, which is essentially a portrait of Christ himself, summons us to follow him in discipleship. By entering into an intimate relationship of friendship and confidence with him, his goodness becomes ours, and this enables us to obey the injunction to be perfect, as our heavenly Father is perfect (see Mt 5:48). The Sermon is also a message of hope, teaching us that in fellowship with Jesus, what is impossible becomes possible. We become capable of fellowship with God and definitive

salvation is offered to us. Eternal life is not utopia and it is
not the expectation of what does not exist: it is the real life,
which has already begun, in communion with Jesus Christ.
As Ratzinger explains, Christian hope has a here and now
quality. When St. Paul affirms that "in this hope we were
saved" (Rom 8:24), he is, in effect, saying that it is not that
salvation will be granted to us but that we are in fact saved
now, even though we do not yet see what we hope for.[14]

3. Love

Hope is born of faith and leads to love. Faith teaches us
that there is a love that is an immense affirmation of my
very existence, while hope is the certainty that I shall receive
this great and indestructible love and that I am already loved
with this love here and now.[15] God loves us not because
we are especially good or particularly virtuous, not because
we are in any way useful or necessary to him, but simply
because he is good.[16]

In his encyclical *Deus Caritas Est*, Pope Benedict XVI
states at the outset that love is at the heart of what it means
to be Christian and that the purpose of the encyclical is
"to speak of the love which God lavishes upon us and
which we in turn must share with others".[17] This, of course,

[14] See Ratzinger, *The Yes of Jesus Christ*, p. 64. Ratzinger bases his explanation on St. Augustine's interpretation of Rom 8:24 (cf. *Contra Faustum*, 11,
7 [PL 42: 251]). On eternal life as a present reality, see also Joseph Ratzinger,
"My Joy Is to Be in Thy Presence", in his *God Is Near Us: The Eucharist, the
Heart of Life* (San Francisco: Ignatius Press, 2003), pp. 130–48.

[15] See Ratzinger, *The Yes of Jesus Christ*, p. 69.

[16] See Joseph Ratzinger, *What It Means to Be a Christian* (San Francisco:
Ignatius Press, 2006), p. 69.

[17] Benedict XVI, Encyclical Letter *Deus Caritas Est*, December 25, 2005,
no. 1 (Vatican City: Libreria Editrice Vaticana, 2006).

is not a new insight for Joseph Ratzinger, but it is typical of his way of expressing what the essence of Christianity is. As early as December 1964, in a series of Advent sermons delivered before university students in Münster, he explained that the Christian is one who loves, and who seeks to love as God loves.[18] Being a Christian means having love. However, if we are honest, we know that we cannot rely on our own possibilities: our love falls short of what is expected of us; it is too frail and we are too selfish. At this point, faith comes to our aid, for it teaches us that God loves us with an abundant love that knows no bounds and that this love will make up for the all too obvious shortcomings of our own love, if we are only humble enough to open our hands to receive it as a gift. In the final analysis, everything we encounter in Christian teaching and dogma is no more than an explanation of the unique, fundamental, decisive, and truly sufficient reality of the love of God and men.[19]

In *The Yes of Jesus Christ*, Ratzinger reflects on the connection between fear, hope, and love and on the nature of love itself. Genuine hope and love involve trusting oneself to the other. There is a kind of fear that necessarily accompanies true love: the fear of hurting the beloved, of destroying the foundations of love through one's own fault. In our age, which has removed anxiety about salvation and sin from

[18] See Ratzinger, *What It Means to Be a Christian*, p. 69.

[19] See ibid., p. 76. In *Introduction to Christianity*, after presenting six principles that summarize what it means to be Christian (the individual and the whole; the principle of "for"; the law of disguise; the law of excess or superfluity; finality and hope; the primacy of acceptance and Christian positivity), Ratzinger identifies love as the center in which they all coalesce, while insisting that love is inseparably connected to faith and hope (see 2nd ed., pp. 243–70, especially pp. 269–70).

man and has thus apparently made him free from fear, new anxieties have taken over, such as fear about technological power or major illnesses, and preoccupation about the emptiness and perceived meaninglessness of existence. These anxieties are masks for the fear of death—alarm at the finiteness of our being.

However, anyone who loves God knows that there is only one real threat for man: the danger of losing God. Whoever abandons God in order to be free from this true fear falls victim to a tyranny of fear without hope. Fear of the Lord, linked as it is to hope and love, is the beginning of wisdom (cf. Ps 111:10), but where it is lacking, people lose their criterion for judging the truth of things and they succumb to fear of man. Making an idol of what is not truth but merely appearance, they make possible every kind of folly.

The encyclical *Deus Caritas Est* strongly emphasizes the connection between natural and supernatural love, as does Ratzinger's earlier book *The Yes of Jesus Christ*. In this regard, his thinking owes much to the reflections of Josef Pieper and consequently to the views of St. Thomas Aquinas, while he completes Pieper's basic insights by drawing on the resources of Sacred Scripture and Patristic thought. The Swedish Lutheran bishop Anders Nygren (1890–1978) had introduced the thesis that supernatural love or agape, characterized by unselfish self-giving, is radically other than natural love or eros, primarily understood as love of a desirous, egocentric kind.[20] A similar distinction is found in the writings of the great Swiss Reformed theologian Karl Barth

---

[20] Nygren presents his thesis on love in *Eros und Agape: Gestaltwandlungen der christlichen Liebe*, 2 vols. (Gütersloh: Verlag C. Bertelsmann, 1930, 1937). For a critical discussion, see Josef Pieper, "On Love", in *Faith, Hope, Love* (San Francisco: Ignatius Press, 1997), pp. 207–18.

(1886–1968), although he is less doctrinaire than Nygren.[21] Such a radical separation is based on an incorrect understanding of the relationship of the orders of creation and redemption, and of nature and grace. Furthermore, it distorts both supernatural and natural love, a purely "supernatural" love, completely distinct from natural love, would be powerless, while natural love, which of its nature is a thirsting after infinite fullness, would be falsified if it were rigidly enclosed within the finite, separated from its dynamic reaching out to the eternal.[22] The general principle that grace presupposes nature applies above all here.

Despite their differences, all forms of love involve an act of fundamental assent to another, of saying yes to the one to whom the love is directed, of rejoicing at the existence of the beloved.[23] As a result, the lover discovers that because the existence of the beloved is good, his own existence has become a better, more precious, and happier one.

Love, as affirmation of the other's existence, is a creative act, a new creation.[24] Apart from physical birth and the satisfying of the basic material requirements of life, the affirmation that love entails is necessary in order to live a full and happy human life. Man needs the approval of another

[21] Barth deals with this issue in vol. 4, part 2, of the *Kirchliche Dogmatik*, in a chapter entitled "The Problem of Human Love"; for a discussion, see Pieper, "On Love", pp. 214–16.

[22] Pope Benedict XVI develops the connection between eros and agape in the first part of the encyclical *Deus Caritas Est*, drawing on Scripture, Church writers, and philosophers; see also Joseph Ratzinger, *In the Beginning: A Catholic Understanding of Creation and the Fall* (Grand Rapids: Eerdmans, 1995), pp. 94–95, and his *The Yes of Jesus Christ*, pp. 88–89; Pieper, "On Love", pp. 216–18.

[23] See Ratzinger, *The Yes of Jesus Christ*, pp. 89–90; Pieper, "On Love", pp. 163–72.

[24] On this point, see also Ratzinger, *In the Beginning*, pp. 98–99.

so as to be able to accept himself. This everyday human experience helps us to understand something of the mysteries of creation and redemption. God's love was the force that created being out of nothing, the real foundation on which all reality is based. His second yes, which was made manifest by Christ's death on the Cross, is our rebirth, making it possible for us to live in a final and definitive way. As people who have been affirmed by God in this way, we are called to share in his yes by giving birth to others in a new way by affirming them through love.[25]

Love, as we saw earlier, is inseparable from truth. The yes of my love for another presupposes that it is truly good that he exists. This is in fact the case, because he is made by God: without a creator God who vouches for the goodness of everything that exists, love would lose its justification and become groundless.[26] Love means saying an unconditional yes to the beloved. We love others, not for this or that quality, but for themselves, with all their strengths and weaknesses. Real love, in contrast to infatuation, directs itself to the truth of the beloved. It is always ready to forgive, but forgiveness presupposes the recognition of sin as sin.[27] The true lover is not indulgent but works for the true happiness of the beloved; this may involve pain and purification for the beloved and is exacting on both lover and beloved. Only love gives the power to forgive and to accompany the other on the path of suffering that transforms.

The Cross of Christ can be understood only when the essential connection between truth and love is grasped:

[25] See Ratzinger, *The Yes of Jesus Christ*, pp. 90–91.

[26] See ibid., p. 93; also Joseph Ratzinger, "Vorfragen zu einer Theologie der Erlösung", in *Erlösung und Emanzipation*, ed. Leo Scheffczyk (Freiburg im Breisgau: Herder, 1973), pp. 141–55.

[27] See Ratzinger, *The Yes of Jesus Christ*, p. 93.

Forgiveness has to do with truth, and for that reason it involves the cross of the Son and it requires our conversion. Forgiveness is indeed the restoration of truth, the renewal of being, and the overcoming of the lie that lurks in every sin: of its nature sin is always a departure from the truth of one's own being and thus from the truth of the creator, God.[28]

The theology of the Cross is in reality a theology of truth and love: the Cross means that Christ goes before us and accompanies us on the painful way that leads to our healing and salvation. All of this has pastoral consequences: a pastoral approach of appeasement stands in glaring contrast to the approach of love. Correct pastoral practice leads to the truth, inspires love for the truth, and helps people to accept the pain of the truth, with a view to their healing: "It must itself be a form of accompanying people on the difficult but beautiful way to new life that is also the way to true and lasting joy." [29]

What of love of self? On the one hand, we are all called to salvation. Each one of us is willed and loved by God, and our highest task is to respond to that love. Since this is so, we have a vocation to happiness. Ratzinger goes so far as to say that to become happy is a "duty" that is both natural and supernatural.[30] On the other hand, Christ speaks in rather strong terms of the necessity of self-denial and of losing one's own life (see Mk 8:35; 10:17–22). In this way, he insists that proper self-affirmation or love of self is possible only if we

[28] Ibid., p. 95.

[29] Ibid., p. 97. On this point, see also Joseph Ratzinger, *God and the World: A Conversation with Peter Seewald* (San Francisco: Ignatius Press, 2002), pp. 186–87.

[30] See Ratzinger, *The Yes of Jesus Christ*, p. 98.

go beyond ourselves and lose ourselves. In doing so, para-doxically, we come to find and love ourselves.

In this context, Ratzinger recalls how impressed he was as a seminarian by the last words of the young priest in Georges Bernanos' great novel *The Diary of a Country Priest*, who, shortly before dying, reflects on how easy it is to hate oneself and on the extraordinary grace of being able to love oneself humbly like any of the suffering members of Jesus Christ.[31] Self-hatred and the inability to accept oneself are all too common. If people cannot stand themselves, they cannot love others.[32] Self-aversion can often accompany self-ishness, since selfishness frequently arises from internal tur-moil. Authentic love of self, which involves the right relation to the self in freedom, grows of itself. While continuous self-seeking leads to dissatisfaction and inability to accept oneself, the yes that is given to me by someone else makes me capable of addressing this yes to myself, in and with the other. In this sense, the "I" is brought to fulfillment by the "thou". Furthermore, only someone who has accepted him-self can address a real yes to someone else. Once again, the connection of love and truth emerges: accepting oneself,

[31] See ibid., pp. 98–99, and Georges Bernanos, *Journal d'un curé de cam-pagne*, in his *Œuvres romanesques*, Bibliothèque de la Pléiade (Paris: Gallimard, 1961), p. 1258. Ratzinger frequently quotes Bernanos; see *Introduction to Chris-tianity*, 2nd ed., p. 280; "Faith as Trust and Joy—Evangelium" in *Principles of Catholic Theology*, p. 79; *The Yes of Jesus Christ*, p. 128, n. 7; *A New Song for the Lord: Faith in Christ and Liturgy* (New York: Crossroad, 1996), p. 213. On Bernanos' understanding of the Christian life, see Joseph Murphy, "Georges Bernanos on the Adventure of Christian Living", in *Irish Theological Quarterly* 69 (2004): 349–75.

[32] Several of Bernanos' characters are consumed by a radical self-hatred, making them incapable of loving others. As an example, Ratzinger cites the abbé Cénabre, who features in *L'Imposture* and *La Joie* (cf. *The Yes of Jesus Christ*, p. 128, n. 7). One could add others, such as Mouchette (*Sous le Soleil de Satan*) and Arsène (*Monsieur Ouine*).

loving oneself, presupposes truth and demands a continuous journeying toward the truth.[33]

Supernatural love builds on the foundations of human
love. Divine love does not destroy human love, but deepens
and radicalizes it. Like every love, supernatural love comes
from a yes that has been given to me. In this case, the yes
comes from God through Christ's yes to us, who had been
alienated from God by our sins. Agape thus presupposes
that Christ's crucified love has somehow become perceptible to us through faith. By contemplating the pierced side
of Christ we come to know what true love is and thus
discover the direction for our own life and love.[34] We have
already seen in the discussion on faith how our faith is made
possible, among other things, by the witness of the saints;
likewise we discover true love through contact with the love
of the saints. If the Lord's yes really penetrates me so that
my soul is reborn, then my own self is saturated with him
and marked by sharing in him (cf. Gal 2:20). A mutual inward
exchange takes place. I am led into the great new "I" of
the body of Christ and made at home in it by the transformation of faith.

This has practical consequences: the other can no longer
be a stranger to me but is part of me. Even though I may
not have a purely human natural attraction for this other
person, I can truly love him by giving him Christ's yes,
which has become my own yes while remaining his. Impelled
by the supernatural love of agape, individual private sym-
pathies and antipathies are replaced by Christ's sympathy,
his compassion, his suffering with people, and his loving

[33] See Ratzinger, *The Yes of Jesus Christ*, p. 100.
[34] See Benedict XVI, *Deus Caritas Est*, no. 12; Ratzinger, *The Yes of Jesus Christ*, p. 101.

with them. Christ's compassion, which has been communicated to me in the life of faith, makes it possible for me to be compassionate toward others. It enables me to bestow on them a yes that is greater than my own, one that enables others to come into contact with the deepest yes that alone gives meaning to every human yes.[35]

Exercising the love of agape requires practice, patience, perseverance, and the acceptance of continual setbacks. It means allowing Christ's yes gradually to penetrate my being and become mine. It involves risk taking and self-denial, but it is this crucifixion of self that leads to a great inner joy, to "resurrection". The more I dare to lose myself in this way, the more I find myself. The Cross is a constant challenge to surrender ourselves into Christ's hands: only in so doing can we become truly free and fulfilled. By patiently and humbly walking with Christ, his yes gradually becomes mine: this is the secret of loving, of holiness, and, we could add, of true joy.[36]

[35] See Ratzinger, *The Yes of Jesus Christ*, p. 103.
[36] See ibid., pp. 103–4.

Chapter IV

THE TRINITY

God's love is the sole motivation for creating all things; with them he wills to share his love and joy. Even the fall of the angels and of man did not prevent God from realizing "the mystery of his will" (Eph 1:9). Through Christ's saving work and the gift of the Holy Spirit, we are restored to friendship with God and come to share in his life, as his adopted children, and therefore in God's own joy.

Joy is based on love and truth, and since God is truth and love, it must be rooted in the Blessed Trinity itself. This conviction underlies Joseph Ratzinger's teaching on joy. Although he does not set out the connection between the Triune God and joy in one place, it may be gleaned from his writings on God, creation, Jesus Christ, and the Holy Spirit.[1] The revelation of the Trinitarian mystery indicates that the ultimate reality is a mystery of loving unity

[1] See especially (1) Ratzinger's, *Introduction to Christianity*, 2nd ed. (San Francisco: Ignatius Press, 2004); (2) his meditations on the Trinity contained in *Der Gott Jesu Christi: Betrachtungen über den Dreieinigen Gott* (Munich: Kösel, 2006); (3) his collection of four homilies on creation and the fall preached during Lent 1981 in the Liebfrauenkirche, Munich, and contained in the volume *In the Beginning: A Catholic Understanding of Creation and the Fall* (Grand

that maintains a distinction of Persons, who are constituted by the intra-Trinitarian relationships. Man is made in the image of the Triune God; he is made for God, he is able to address him, and, by looking to God, he learns that true love, which gives rise to genuine and lasting joy, involves living in a relational way from others and for them.

Joy flows from knowing that God truly cares for us and can be invoked by us in prayer. It is thus intimately linked with knowing that God is a personal God, a God who is not hidden but who has revealed his name so that he may be addressed. God, without prejudice to his oneness, is in reality a communion of Persons bound in love. This truth is revealed in the fullness of time through the saving missions of the Son and the Holy Spirit. The New Testament revelation of the Blessed Trinity helps us to understand what love ultimately is, and since joy is based on love and truth, Christian belief in the Trinity also has something to teach us about joy itself.

1. The name of God

An examination of the biblical theme of the "name" of God reveals what is special about Israel's grasp of God and consequently about the God of Jesus Christ.[2] The central text of the Old Testament in this regard is the story of the burning bush (see Ex 3), in which God makes his name known to Moses, thus providing the foundations for Israel's

---

Rapids: Eerdmans, 1995). For bibliography on Christ and the Holy Spirit, see chapter 6, n. 5 and chapter 7, n. 1, respectively.

[2] See Ratzinger, *Introduction to Christianity*, pp. 116–36, 151–90; also Ratzinger, *Der Gott Jesu Christi*, pp. 13–85. Joseph Ratzinger, *Jesus of Nazareth: From the Baptism in the Jordan to the Transfiguration* (New York: Doubleday, 2007), pp. 142–45.

understanding of who God is. God reveals himself to be "the God of your father, the God of Abraham, the God of Isaac, and the God of Jacob" (Ex 3:6), before declaring that he has seen the oppression of his people and is sending Moses to Pharaoh to lead the "sons of Israel" out of Egypt (Ex 3:10). Moses asks for clear knowledge of God and proof of his authority:

> Moses said to God, "If I come to the sons of Israel and say to them, 'The God of your fathers has sent me to you,' and they ask me, 'What is his name?' what shall I say to them?" God said to Moses, "I AM WHO I AM ['ehyeh 'asher 'ehyeh]." And he said, "Say this to the sons of Israel, 'I AM has sent me to you.'" God also said to Moses, "Say this to the sons of Israel, 'The Lord [Yahweh], the God of your fathers, the God of Abraham, the God of Isaac, and the God of Jacob, has sent me to you': this is my name for ever, and thus I am to be remembered throughout all generations. (Ex 3:13–15)

According to Ratzinger, the aim of this text is to establish the name "Yahweh" as the definitive name of God in Israel "by anchoring it historically in the origins of Israel's nationhood and the sealing of the covenant" and "by giving it a meaning".[3] With regard to the meaning, the incomprehensible word "Yahweh" is traced back to the root *hayah*, "to be". While this is possible from the point of view of the Hebrew consonant system, it is debatable whether it corresponds philologically with the real origin of the name "Yahweh". What matters, however, is not so much the original linguistic sense as giving it a meaning here and now. As Ratzinger explains:

---

[3] Ratzinger, *Introduction to Christianity*, p. 117.

The etymology is in reality a means of establishing a meaningful attitude. This illumination of the name "Yahweh"
by the little word "Being" (I AM) is accompanied by a second attempt at clarification consisting of the statement that
Yahweh is the God of (Israel's) fathers, the God of Abraham, Isaac, and Jacob. This means that the concept of "Yahweh" is to be enlarged and deepened by the equation of
the God so described with the God of Israel's fathers, a
God who had probably been addressed for the most part by
the names El and Elohim.[4]

The Septuagint translators of the Hebrew Bible, influenced by Greek philosophy, identified the biblical name for
God with the philosophical understanding of God as being,
thus wedding belief to ontology. Their interpretation influenced the Church Fathers. However, to the philosophical
thinker, there is something scandalous about being able to
give a name to the biblical God. After all, one could not
have given a name to the Platonic "Being" and referred to
it by this name as a kind of individual. Could it be that
since we can name the God of Israel, we are dealing with
a fundamentally different conception? The gap between
the Platonic Being and the God of the Bible seems to
widen further because the Platonic, absolute Being is not
named and it does not name itself, while it is clear from the
Exodus text that we can name God only because he has
named himself. Given this, some exegetes and theologians
reject the Septuagint and patristic interpretation as based on
a misunderstanding.

While it is practically impossible to ascertain the original meaning of "Yahweh" according to its etymological
origin, it does seem clear that the full form of the name

---

[4] Ibid., pp. 117–18.

"Yahweh" first occurs in Israel: "Its development seems to be the work of Israel's faith, which, not without models but creatively transforming them, here molded its own name for God and, in this name, its own figure of God." [5] Ratzinger maintains that there is good reason to suppose that the formation of the name was the deed of Moses, who with it brought new hope to his oppressed fellow countrymen. Israel became a people, thanks to God; she came to be herself "through the call of hope signified by the name of God". [6]

It is possible that the name "Yahweh" bears some relation to Babylonian names containing references to God formed from the word *yaun* or containing the syllable *yau* or *ya*, which has more or less the meaning "mine" or "my God". This word formation refers to the personal God, the God "who is concerned with man and is himself personal or person-centered". [7] This links up with the God-figure described in the Bible as the "God of our fathers". The suggested etymology would thus fit in exactly with the story of the burning bush, "itself described as the inner assumption of the Yahweh-faith with the faith of (Israel's) fathers, with the God of Abraham, Isaac, and Jacob". [8]

When the patriarchs referred to the "God of the fathers" as "El" or "Elohim", they made use of the El-religion of the surrounding peoples, which emphasized the social and personal character of the divinity. Rather than seeing God as tied to a particular holy place, they understood the "God of the fathers" to be a personal God who is present and powerful wherever man is. God is a "personal and person-centered

[5] Ibid., pp. 120–21.
[6] Ibid., p. 121.
[7] Ibid.
[8] Ibid., p. 122.

God, who is to be thought of and found on the plane of I and You, not primarily in holy places".[9] This God is not just some power or other, effective in a particular place, but the power "which embraces in itself all power and stands above all individual powers".[10]

As Abraham and the other patriarchs came to realize, God is the God of the promise: he is not a force of nature or a God who orients man to the recurring pattern of the cosmic cycle, but One who directs man's attention to coming events, to a meaning and goal that have a final validity. In short, "he is regarded as the God of hope in the future, in a direction that is irreversible."[11]

Something of God's transcendence emerges in the gradual abandonment of the singular "El" in favor of the plural "Elohim". God "is one, but as the exceedingly great, entirely Other, he himself transcends the bounds of singular and plural; he lies beyond them".[12] God cannot simply be fitted into our categories of singular and plural. He is truly one, but he is also everything divine. All of this prepares for the definitive revelation of the mystery of God as Trinity.

God's answer to Moses' request to reveal his name seems to be a rebuff, a refusal to give a name, as is indicated elsewhere by his refusal to reveal his name when asked to do so by Jacob (see Gen 32:29) and Manoah (see Judg 13:18). He is not like the gods of the surrounding nations, who are individual gods alongside other similar gods, and who therefore need a name. The explanation of the mysterious name "Yahweh" by the verb "am" serves as a kind of negative theology, withdrawing us from the world of what is well

[9] Ibid., p. 124.
[10] Ibid.
[11] Ibid.
[12] Ibid., p. 125.

known, which the name seems to be, into the hidden and unknown: "It dissolves the name into mystery, so that the familiarity and unfamiliarity of God, concealment and revelation, are indicated simultaneously." [13]

Yet, despite the mystery surrounding the name, Moses was authorized to say to those who might question him: "I AM has sent me to you" (Ex 3:14). God does give an answer, even if it is a riddle. Most contemporary biblical scholars see in the phrase the expression of helpful proximity: God does not reveal his nature as it is in itself but he does reveal himself as a God for Israel, a God for man. It may be that it indicates God as the one who causes to be and even as "he who is". The French exegete Edmond Jacob, appealing to the theology of Deutero-Isaiah (cf. Is 40:6–8), sees the name "Yahweh" as indicating endurance and presence, Being in contrast to Becoming, as that which abides and persists in all passing away. [14] The God who "is" is, at the same time, the God who is with us.

The episode of the burning bush should not be interpreted in isolation. It is to be understood primarily against the background of a world saturated with gods, "in which it makes Israel's faith visible, both in its continuity and in its efforts to differentiate itself, and at the same time develops it further by adding the many-faceted idea of Being as an intellectual element". [15]

The process of interpretation did not end with the story of the burning bush but was carried further, especially by the prophets, among whom Ezekiel and Deutero-Isaiah stand out. Deutero-Isaiah makes it clear that the God of Israel is

[13] Ibid., p. 128.
[14] See ibid., p. 129.
[15] Ibid., p. 130.

not one god among others but the only God, who alone
endures, while the powers of this world collapse and disappear (see Is 41:4; 43:1–28; 44:6; 48:12). The Septuagint
translates the mysterious "I am He" of Isaiah 48:12 by *egō
eimi*. This name, as Deutero-Isaiah uses it, contains a message of hope and confidence: God is the one who *is*, in
contrast to the Babylonian gods who have been toppled
over and pass away.

This brings us to the New Testament and in particular to
St. John's Gospel, which has as one of its primary themes
the revelation of the name of God. John makes the "I am"
of Isaiah into the central formula of his faith in God, but
he does so by making it the key expression of his Christology:

> The formula that first occurs in the episode of the burning
> bush, that at the end of the Exile becomes the expression
> of hope and certainty in face of the declining gods and
> depicts Yahweh's lasting victory over all these powers, now
> finds itself here, too, at the center of the faith, but through
> becoming testimony to Jesus of Nazareth.[16]

Jesus himself makes use of the "I am" formula on various occasions, most unambiguously in the discussion on
Abraham (see Jn 8:58). John also compares Jesus to Moses,
in order to demonstrate Jesus' superiority over the Old Testament figure (see Jn 1:17; 3:14; 6:32; 9:29).

John 17, the so-called "high priestly prayer" of Jesus, is,
in Joseph Ratzinger's view, perhaps the heart of the fourth
Gospel.[17] It is the New Testament counterpart to the story
of the burning bush; indeed, Jesus is the one in whom this
story first attains its full meaning. In this chapter, the theme

[16] Ibid., p. 132; on the Johannine "I am", see also Ratzinger, *Jesus of Nazareth*, pp. 345–55.
[17] See Ratzinger, *Introduction to Christianity*, p. 132.

of God's name recurs like a *leitmotiv* (vv. 6, 11, 12, 26). Jesus appears, so to speak, as the burning bush, from which the name of God is revealed to mankind, enabling us to invoke him and establish a relationship with him. But since he also applies to himself the "I am" of Exodus 3 and Deutero-Isaiah, it becomes clear, at the same time, that "*he himself* is the name, that is, the 'invocability' of God."[18] The idea of the name of God thus enters a decisive new phase: the name is no longer a word but a person, namely, Jesus himself.

Why is this discussion on the name of God so significant?[19] To understand this, one must distinguish, as Ratzinger does, between names and concepts. While the concept seeks to grasp the nature of a thing as it is in itself, the name, while it should fit the thing it names, is concerned above all with making it possible to invoke the thing, to establish a relationship with it. A man's name enables me to call on him, to embrace him within the structure of social relations and to establish a relationship of fellow humanity.[20]

When God names himself, he makes it possible for us to call upon him, and in doing so he enters into a relationship with us; he is "there" for us. St. John presents Jesus Christ as the real, living name of God. In him, the meaning of the

[18] Ibid., p. 133.

[19] See ibid., pp. 133–35.

[20] In this, a name differs from a number. It is not insignificant that the beast of the Book of Revelation does not have a name but a number (see Rev 13:18). In the concentration camps, the assigning of a number to each prisoner was designed to eliminate the person's identity and history, reducing him to a mere cog or function in a gigantic machine. In today's computerized world, there is a risk of reducing the person to function, regarding only what can be expressed in numbers as important, while disregarding everything else; see Ratzinger, *Der Gott Jesu Christi*, pp. 28–30.

discussion on the name of God has reached its goal: in him, "God has really become he who can be invoked" and has entered forever into coexistence with us.[21]

The biblical notion of God is careful to balance two aspects. On the one hand, he is a personal God, with all that entails: proximity, the possibility of being invoked, self-bestowal. This aspect is expressed in the idea of the "God of our fathers" and later in that of "the God of Jesus Christ". On the other hand, this accessibility is the free gift of the One "who is beyond space and time, bound to nothing and binding everything to himself".[22] This aspect is emphasized in the idea of God as being and in the enigmatic "I AM". Israel's God is not the God of one people, but the one true God. Biblical faith in God is paradoxical in its combination of the two aspects, in the fact that Being is accepted as a Person and the Person is accepted as Being itself, that "only what is hidden is accepted as the One who is near, only the inaccessible as the One who is accessible, the one (*das Eine*) as the One (*der Eine*) who exists for all men and for whom all exist".[23]

2. The Trinity of love

The biblical revelation of God shows not only that God is personal and that he can be invoked by man, but also that he is tri-personal. Though one in essence, God is three Persons. In the mystery of the Blessed Trinity, we discover the highest form of unity in love, which draws man into its embrace.

---

[21] Ratzinger, *Introduction to Christianity*, p. 135; see also Ratzinger, *Jesus of Nazareth*, pp. 143–44.

[22] Ratzinger, *Introduction to Christianity*, p. 135 (slightly modified).

[23] Ibid., p. 136.

Faith in the Trinitarian God of love is the distinguishing mark of Christianity. Every day, we make the sign of the cross, perhaps all too hurriedly and distractedly, as a reminder of our baptism into the Trinitarian faith of the Church. Unfortunately, however, for many of us the mystery of the Trinity (three Persons, one God) seems distant, an abstract formulation to which we willingly subscribe but which impinges little on our everyday life.

Conscious of this difficulty, Joseph Ratzinger's discussion on the mystery of the Trinity, while respecting our inability fully to comprehend it, aims at presenting it in such a way that it emerges as firmly grounded in the experience of the first Christians and becomes a vital reality for our lives today.[24]

The formulation of the Trinitarian dogma was not the result of philosophical speculation on the mystery of God but originated in an effort to digest historical experiences. The biblical faith of the Old Testament was concerned with God, encountered as the Father of Israel, the Father of the peoples, the Creator and Lord of the world. The coming of Jesus Christ was a completely unexpected event in which God showed himself from a hitherto unknown side. Christ is truly man, but he knows and professes himself to be the Son of God. He is "sent" from God, yet he is completely God; he is not an intermediary being, yet he addresses God as "Father", which means that he must be other than the Father. At the same time, he is Emmanuel, "God with us", God in human form and nature. It turns out that as mediator, he must be both God himself and "man himself"; otherwise, he would be leading us not to God but away from him. In him, God meets

---

[24] See especially Ratzinger, *Introduction to Christianity*, pp. 162–90; Ratzinger, *Der Gott Jesu Christi*, pp. 33–53.

me "not as Father, but as Son and as my brother, whereby—both incomprehensibly and quite comprehensibly—a duality appears in God: God as 'I' and 'You' in one".[25]

This new experience of God was followed by another: the experience of the Holy Spirit, the presence of God in our innermost being. Again, it turns out that the Spirit is not simply identical either with the Father or the Son, nor is he yet a third thing erected between God and us; rather, the Spirit "is the manner in which God gives himself to us, in which he enters into us, so that he is *in* man yet, in the midst of this 'indwelling', is infinitely *above* him".[26]

The dogma of the Trinity was gradually developed in the course of the early centuries of the Church's history in an effort to reconcile these truths. In formulating it, an essential question was whether man in his relations with God "is only dealing with the reflections of his own consciousness or whether it is given to him to reach out beyond himself and to encounter God himself".[27] The reply to this would have obvious consequences for man's ability to speak correctly about God and to worship him and pray to him. Given the importance of these issues, one can understand why the early Church discussions regarding the correct formulation of the mystery of God were so heated and passionate. Finally, the path of faith won out: God truly *is* as he *shows* himself.[28] The New Testament attests not only that God acts in our favor in a humanly comprehensible way, but also that he enables us to know him as he is in himself.[29]

---

[25] Ratzinger, *Introduction to Christianity*, p. 164.

[26] Ibid.

[27] Ibid.

[28] See ibid., p. 165.

[29] One could express this in more technical terms: the economic Trinity is the immanent Trinity; for a discussion, see Luis F. Ladaria, "La relazione

The orthodox Christian belief in God was established at the Councils of Nicaea I in 325 and Constantinople I in 381. This faith came to be expressed in a formula used in a letter of the Synod of Constantinople of 382 to Pope Damasus, which owes much to the teaching of the fourth-century Cappadocian Fathers—Basil the Great, Gregory of Nazianzus, and Gregory of Nyssa—that God is one essence (*ousia*) and three Persons (*prosōpa*) or hypostases.[30] In employing this formula, the Church does not attempt to provide an exhaustive explanation of what God is in himself but seeks to preserve all the elements of a mystery that cannot be plumbed by man.

In classical Greece, the word *prosōpon* meant an actor's mask, and, by extension, his role. When the third-century heretic Sabellius spoke of three divine *prosōpa*, he understood the term in this original sense, implying that the divine Persons are no more than roles whereby the one God manifests himself. For this reason, Basil was reluctant to use the term, but Gregory of Nazianzus allowed it, provided it was not interpreted in Sabellian terms.[31] In orthodox usage, it had to mean something more than this, in order to express the truth that the Son is other than the Father. The struggle to arrive at an adequate understanding of "person" in order to safeguard Christian faith in God did not happen immediately, but when it did, it was also applied to the individual of the human species, thereby provoking a major revolution in man's understanding of himself. For the

tra la Trinità economica e la Trinità immanente", in his *La Trinità mistero di comunione* (Milan: Figlie di San Paolo, 2002), pp. 13–86.

[30] For the text, see *Conciliorum Oecumenicorum Decreta*, ed. G. Alberigo et al. (Bologna: Edizioni Dehoniane, 1996), p. 28.

[31] See Edmund J. Fortman, *The Triune God: A Historical Study of the Doctrine of the Trinity* (Grand Rapids: Baker Books, 1982), p. 79.

moment, however, the term *prosōpon* (or *persona* in Latin, a term introduced by Tertullian) was used in the profession of Trinitarian faith to safeguard the fullness of the mystery of God as he revealed himself.

This profession of faith is, says Ratzinger, "the only real way to renounce the arrogance of 'knowing all about it', which makes smooth solutions with their false modesty so tempting".[32] To illustrate the point, he refers to the inadequacies of two early Christian approaches to the mystery of God: Subordinationism and Monarchianism.[33]

Subordinationism in its various forms sees Christ as dependent on the Father and thus as inferior to him. As a result,

---

[32] Ratzinger, *Introduction to Christianity*, p. 168.

[33] Monarchianism aimed at defending the oneness of God. Its heretical forms include Adoptionism and Modalism. Adoptionists, such as the Ebionites, held that since there is only one God, Christ is simply a man adopted by God and raised by him to a special dignity as Son of God. In general, Modalism maintained that there are not really three distinct Persons in God: when we speak of the Father, the Son, and the Holy Spirit, we are simply referring to three different ways or modes in which the one God relates to the world. A version of this is Patripassionism, which affirmed that Christ is the same as the Father, who became man in order to suffer. Sabellianism is closely related to these modalist positions. Sabellius, whose teaching was condemned around 220 by Pope Callixtus, seems to have held that there is in God one *hypostasis* and three *prosōpa*, by which he meant roles or modes of revelation. According to him, God revealed himself as Father in creation, as Son in the redemption, and as the Holy Spirit in works of sanctification. In contrast, Subordinationism emphasized that the Son and Holy Spirit are distinct from the Father and that the Father enjoys priority over the other two Persons. In its heretical versions, it denied the true divinity of the Son and the Holy Spirit, seeing them as creatures. Arianism maintained that the Logos is not truly God but a creature generated before all others. The various kinds of Semi-Arianism saw the Logos as similar to the Father, but they rejected the Nicene teaching of consubstantiality, asserting that this teaching lent support to the views of Sabellius, which had been condemned. The Macedonians, a sect of the Semi-Arians, held that the Holy Spirit is merely a creature; their heresy was combated by St. Athanasius and the Cappadocian Fathers, before being condemned at Constantinople I in 381 and by Pope St. Damasus in 382.

Christ cannot be God, but a (created) being particularly close to God. Were this the case, Christ could not be the mediator between God and man. Hence, man would be cut off from God himself and would remain confined to the antechamber, so to speak, having to deal with God's ministers rather than God himself. However, anyone who really believes in the Lordship of God "will have to hold fast to the belief that God *is* man, that the being of God and man intermingle, and will thus adopt with the belief in Christ the starting point of the doctrine of the Trinity".[34]

Monarchianism, in contrast, maintains that we do encounter God, but, in its modalist version, it sees the Father, Son, and Holy Spirit merely as masks or roles (*prosōpa* in the original sense) of the one God. According to this doctrine, divine revelation teaches us something about ourselves and about how God manifests himself in history, but nothing about how God truly is in himself. Consequently, man fails to penetrate God's own reality. In this way, Monarchianism eliminates the personal element in God, the encounter of freedoms and the dialogue of love. All is merged into the inevitability of the one process of reason.[35]

The formulation of the dogma of the Trinity is, in part, an exercise in negative theology, emphasizing the insolubility of the mystery of God.[36] The basic concepts used to express this mystery are inadequate but acceptable as "poor stammering utterances".[37] In this, we are reminded of

[34] Ratzinger, *Introduction to Christianity*, p. 168.

[35] Monarchianism was resurrected and transformed in the nineteenth century in the thought of G. W. F. Hegel and Friedrich Schelling, for whom the process of God's self-manifestation in history becomes the process of God himself.

[36] See Ratzinger, *Introduction to Christianity*, pp. 171–77.

[37] Ibid., p. 172.

St. Augustine, who was well aware of the limitations of the
term "*persona*" but accepted it, since there is no more suitable way of expressing the mystery: "If one asks: 'what are
the Three?', human speech suffers seriously from a great
lack of resources. Nevertheless, the reply was given: 'three
persons', not in order to express that thing, but so as not to
remain silent." [38]

To gain some understanding of the mystery of the Trinity, as well as of what can and cannot be said about God,
we need to bear in mind the tortured history of the formulation of the Trinitarian doctrine in the face of the great
variety of heresies that afflicted the life of the early Church.
Affirmative theological language about God is always subject to correction, because he is always greater than anything we can think of and so we cannot reduce him to our
mental world. At the same time, although the terminology
used to express this mystery is imperfect, it does enable us
to make true statements about God that are necessary for
safeguarding the Church's faith and her life of prayer and
worship. [39]

Furthermore, the formula "one essence, three Persons"
has significant implications for an adequate grasp of what
the person is and what love is. In his *Introduction to Christianity*, Joseph Ratzinger sets these out in three theses, which

[38] St. Augustine, *De Trinitate*, 5, 9, 10 (CCSL 50: 217): "Tamen cum quaeri-
tur quid Tres, magna prorsus inopia humanum laborat eloquium. Dictum est
tamen 'tres personae', non ut illud diceretur, sed ne taceretur."

[39] St. Thomas Aquinas' treatment of the divine names is the classic source
for any discussion on the significance of theological language. For an insight-
ful treatment of his views, see Gregory P. Rocca, *Speaking the Incomprehensible
God: Thomas Aquinas on the Interplay of Positive and Negative Theology* (Washington, D.C.: Catholic University of America Press, 2004); also Thierry-
Dominique Humbrecht, *Théologie négative et noms divins chez saint Thomas
d'Aquin* (Paris: Vrin, 2005).

emphasize the importance of the category of relatedness as the key to understanding both.[40]

The first has to do with the value of unity and plurality. To the classical Greek mind, only unity or oneness is divine, and plurality is a disintegration of unity, a falling away from it. However, the Christian confession of faith in God as simultaneously one and three means that the divinity lies beyond our categories of unity and plurality, as the later Old Testament writers dimly perceived in their application of the plural form "Elohim" to God. God is both one and fullness. Unity and plurality are both grounded in God. Plurality is no longer to be considered a form of disintegration that arises once we leave the world of the divinity nor does it derive from the conflict of two opposing powers, as Manicheism and other dualistic philosophies would hold. Instead, it corresponds to the creative fullness of God, who is above unity and plurality, somehow encompassing both. Belief in the Trinity, which recognizes the plural in the unity of God, provides a definitive basis for the positive validation of the many. Furthermore, the highest unity is not the unity of inflexible monotony, but the unity embracing the plurality of Persons. Consequently, the model of unity towards which created reality strives is not the unity of the atom (where "atom" is understood in its original sense as the smallest indivisible unit), but the unity of Persons related to one another by love. For this reason, "pure oneness can only occur in the spirit and embraces the relatedness of love."[41]

The second sees the formula "one essence, three Persons" as an intrinsic implication of the concept of person.

---

[40] See Ratzinger, *Introduction to Christianity*, pp. 178–90.
[41] Ibid., p. 188.

To confess God as person, which implies that he is knowledge, word, and love, is to acknowledge him as relatedness, as communicability, as fruitfulness. An absolute One who is not related to anyone else and cannot be related to anyone else cannot be personal. If the absolute is personal, it is not an absolute singular. The overstepping of the singular is implied in the concept of person: the Greek word *prosōpon* literally means "look toward", while the Latin *persona* literally means "sounding through"; both express relatedness. In this context, Ratzinger reintroduces the corrective of negative theology, pointing out that "the acknowledgment that God is a person in the guise of a triple personality explodes the naïve, anthropomorphic concept of person."[42] The personality of God infinitely exceeds the human kind of personality, indicating once again the limitations of the notion of person when applied to God.

The third, following on from the second, stresses the importance of the notion of relation in connection with that of person. While the corrective of negative theology must always be applied, it can be affirmed that when we speak about God, we can make some contact with the divine reality and express certain truths about him. The notion of "person" emerged in the attempt to express correctly the mysteries of the Trinity and the Incarnation. Once it was established that God is only One, that there is not a plurality of divine principles, it was clear that the oneness has to lie on the level of substance. Consequently, the threeness that must also be mentioned is not to be sought there, but on a different level, namely, that of relation.

The discovery of dialogue within God, evidenced by such Old Testament passages as Genesis 1:26 and Psalm 110:1, as

[42] Ibid., p. 180.

well as by Jesus' conversations with the Father, as reported
by the evangelists, led to the assumption of the presence in
God of an "I" and a "You", an element of relationship, of
coexistent diversity and affinity, for which the notion of person absolutely dictated itself. In this way, it acquired, beyond
its theatrical and literary significance, a deeper meaning, without losing the vagueness that made it suitable for such a use.[43]

Given this, the notion of relation, which Aristotle had
classified among the "accidents" of a thing, acquires a new
significance in Christian thinking. Dialogue and relation in
God stand beside substance as equally primordial forms of
being. God as substance or "being" is absolutely one. If we
speak of him using the category of triplicity, this does not
imply any multiplication of substance. Rather, it means that
in the one and indivisible God there exists the phenomenon of dialogue, the reciprocal exchange of word and love.
The three Persons are the reality of word and love in their
attachment to each other. They are not substances or per-
sonalities in the modern sense, but the relatedness "whose
pure actuality ... does not impair the unity of the highest
being but fills it out".[44]

"Person" turns out to be nothing other than the pure
relation of being referred to another (*die reine Relation der
Bezogenheit*). Thus, "Father" is purely a concept of relationship. As Augustine puts it: "He is not called Father with
relation to himself but only in relation to the Son; seen by
himself he is simply God." [45] Relationship is not something

---

[43] Ratzinger develops these ideas further in "Concerning the Notion of
Person in Theology", in *Communio* (American ed.) 17 (1990): 439–54. This
article was originally published in 1966.

[44] Ratzinger, *Introduction to Christianity*, p. 183.

[45] St. Augustine, *Enarratio in Psalmum* 68, p. 1, 5 (CCSL 39: 905), as cited
by Ratzinger in *Introduction to Christianity*, p. 183.

added to the person, as with us; person only exists at all as relatedness. The first Person does not beget the Son as though the act of begetting were subsequent to the Person; rather, he *is* the act of begetting, of giving himself, of streaming forth. It is clear, then, that both substance and relation must be considered primordial realities: in this, there lies concealed a revolution in man's view of the world.

These ideas, though seemingly highly speculative, are present in St. John's Gospel, even if expressed differently, and have important consequences for Christian living. In John 5, Jesus says of himself: "The Son can do nothing of his own accord" (v. 19; see v. 30). The name "Son" indicates a relation: this name points away from Jesus and beyond him. Later in the Gospel, Jesus says: "I and the Father are one" (10:30), which initially seems to contradict the earlier statement. On closer examination, however, they turn out to be complementary: "In that Jesus is called 'Son' and is thereby made 'relative' to the Father, and in that Christology is ratified as a statement of relation, the automatic result is the total reference of Christ back to the Father." [46] As the Son, Christ does not exist from or for himself; he exists in the Father and is always one with him.

The Gospel extends these ideas to Christians. Jesus tells the disciples: "Apart from me you can do nothing" (Jn 15:5). Christian existence is placed with Christ in the category of relation. Paralleling the logic that makes Christ say: "I and the Father are one", we find in the priestly prayer the petition "that they may be one, even as we are one" (Jn 17:11, 22). This, however, is a prayer, not a description of a situation that already obtains. To John the evangelist, being a Christian means being like the Son, becoming a son, that

---

[46] Ratzinger, *Introduction to Christianity*, p. 185.

is, not living a self-sufficient and closed existence, but in an open fashion, in the "from" and "toward" characteristic of the Son's relation to the Father.[47] It is in the nature of Christian existence to receive and live life as relatedness and in this way to enter into the unity of God that is the ground of all reality and sustains it. Ratzinger draws out the ecumenical consequences of all this: the lack of being at one with one another arises from a concealed lack of Christliness, of being at one with Christ, and from a clinging to individuality that hinders the coalescence into unity.[48]

The same emphasis on relatedness as the form of Christian existence is found in the Johannine ideas of "mission" and the Word. Jesus is the one "sent" by the Father as his ambassador; he is at one with the Father and absolutely open to the Father's will, without reservation. Jesus, in turn, sends the disciples (see Jn 13:20; 17:18; 20:21), whose work must be characterized by the same unity and unreserved openness. By referring to Jesus as the Word, or Logos, John draws attention to a theme found in Greek and Jewish thought. "Logos" not only signifies the eternal rationality of being, as in classical Greek thought, but also characterizes the man Jesus as the Word that is spoken. This, once again, indicates that Jesus' whole being exists in relation to the One who speaks the Word.

Ratzinger ends with St. Augustine's interpretation of John 7:16, where Jesus says: "My teaching is not mine, but his who sent me." Augustine uses this statement to illustrate the paradoxical nature of the Christian image of God and of Christian existence. Jesus Christ is the Word, and so it is clear that his teaching is himself. The verse then comes to

[47] See ibid., p. 187.
[48] See ibid.

mean: I am by no means just I; I am not mine at all; my I is that of another. Once again, the relatedness at the heart of the doctrine of God and of human existence comes to the fore. As Augustine puts it, "What is so much yours as yourself, and what is so little yours as yourself?"[49] Our own "I" is both what most belongs to us and what least belongs to us, since we neither have it from ourselves nor for ourselves. The category of substance is not sufficient to grasp the mystery of being, particularly of being that knows itself. Such being understands that in being itself it does not belong to itself, "that it only comes to itself by moving away from itself and finding its way back through related-ness to its true primordial state".[50]

Although he is well aware that the doctrine of the Trin-ity remains utterly mysterious, Joseph Ratzinger, by refer-ence to the categories of relatedness, dialogue, self-giving, and love, indicates how it sheds new light on our under-standing of God, created reality, and Christian existence. What is most speculative ends up being most practical: talk-ing about God discloses who man is and where the ulti-mate source of his joy is to be found, and our faltering attempts to express the mystery of God traces out a pro-gram for Christian living, which is both demanding and joyful.

[49] St. Augustine, *In Ioannis Evangelium tractatus* 29, 3 (CCSL 36: 285), as quoted by Ratzinger in *Introduction to Christianity*, p. 190.

[50] Ratzinger, *Introduction to Christianity*, p. 190. The notion of person described here owes much to Patristic thought, especially to Maximus the Confessor; see Hans Urs von Balthasar, *Cosmic Liturgy: The Universe According to Maximus the Confessor* (San Francisco: Ignatius Press, 2003), pp. 235–55. In developing his understanding of person, Ratzinger is also indebted to Hed-wig Conrad-Martius, *Das Sein* (Munich: Kösel, 1957).

Chapter V

CREATION

For Joseph Ratzinger, the Christian profession of faith in God as creator, inherited from the faith of Israel, is of crucial importance, since it tells us who God is and who we are. This belief implies that Christianity has something to say about reality as a whole: the world is not a product of mere chance nor can it be explained solely in terms of an evolutionary process. Instead, it is ultimately dependent on the creative mind of God. He holds history and all peoples in his hands because he is the creator of all things and the source of all power.[1]

At the time of the Exile in Babylon, Israel's awareness that God is the creator of all became sharply focused. Over against him at the beginning, there is only the void. There is no primordial struggle with demonic powers, such as we find in the Babylonian creation myth *Enuma Elish*. For Israel, the world owes its origin solely to God's reason and love. This belief was the decisive "enlightenment" of history. By

[1] See Joseph Ratzinger, *In the Beginning: A Catholic Understanding of Creation and the Fall* (Grand Rapids: Eerdmans, 1995), p. 12. On the question of the relation of creation and evolution, with particular reference to the theories of Jacques Monod, see ibid., pp. 50–58.

placing the world in the context of reason, it enabled people to overcome their fears regarding demonic forces and it
set human reason "firmly on the primordial basis of God's
creating Reason, in order to establish it in truth and in love,
without which an 'enlightenment' would be exorbitant and
utterly foolish".[2] If the world ultimately owes its origins to
reason, then human reason itself is set on a solid basis of
rationality.

Israel's belief in creation was expressed in various ways in
the Old Testament, especially in the first two chapters of
Genesis, in some of the Psalms, and in the Wisdom litera-
ture,[3] but the conclusive and normative scriptural account is
found at the beginning of St. John's Gospel: "In the beginning was the Word, and the Word was with God, and the
Word was God. . . . All things were made through him, and
without him was not anything made that was made" (1:1, 3).[4]

Difficulties arose concerning the belief in creation when
the older texts were read in isolation from the others, and
a certain literal-mindedness began to prevail about particular details, such as the Genesis account of the creation in
six days. This in time led to a conflict between the natural
sciences and theology, which has up to our own day been

[2] Ibid., p. 14.

[3] For a brief account, see the articles "Creation", in *Dictionary of Biblical
Theology*, ed. Xavier Léon-Dufour, 2nd ed. (London: Geoffrey Chapman,
1988), pp. 98–102, and "Création", in *Dictionnaire encyclopédique de la Bible*,
ed. Centre Informatique et Bible, Abbaye de Maredsous, 3rd ed. (Turnhout:
Brepols, 2002), pp. 317–20.

[4] Against the tendency to read Scriptural texts in isolation, Ratzinger here
emphasizes the unity of Scripture. He develops the point that Christology
provides the ultimate criterion for a Christian reading of Scripture: it must
be read as a unity with Christ, as directed to Christ, and through Christ
(see *In the Beginning*, pp. 15–18). On this, see *Catechism of the Catholic Church*,
nos. 128–30.

a burden for the faith. However, this conflict need not have arisen. Faith in creation is reasonable and, even from the point of view of the natural sciences, it remains the "better hypothesis", offering a fuller and better explanation than any of the other theories.[5] The reasonableness of creation "derives from God's Reason and there is no other really convincing explanation".[6] Today, as in the time of Aristotle, the reasonableness of the universe provides us with access to God's Reason: "God himself shines through the reasonableness of his creation"[7] and "the Bible is and continues to be the true 'enlightenment' which has given the world over to human reason and not to exploitation by human beings, because it opened reason to God's truth and love."[8] The biblical creation accounts use images and symbols to speak about reality in a manner that differs from physics and biology: they do not depict the process of becoming nor do they describe the mathematical structure of matter. Instead, "they say in different ways that there is only *one* God and that the universe is not the scene of a struggle among dark forces but rather the creation of his Word."[9]

There is a tendency among some modern theologians to jettison the traditional proofs for the existence of God on account of their shortcomings. Such an approach could lead to the ignoring of the substantial question underlying this discussion, namely, the reasonableness of faith in creation, which in turn would provoke the dissolution of the bond between faith and reason. As a consequence, faith would

[5] For a development of this point, see Ratzinger, *In the Beginning*, pp. 22–25.
[6] Ibid., p. 17.

[7] Ibid., p. 24; cf. Joseph Ratzinger, *Introduction to Christianity*, 2nd ed. (San Francisco: Ignatius Press, 2004), p. 256.

[8] Ratzinger, *In the Beginning*, p. 18.

[9] Ibid., p. 25.

be reduced to merely one of the many human traditions; truth would become folklore. Given this danger, Ratzinger insists that the connection between faith and reason must be maintained: the joy of the faith, he concludes, depends on being aware that faith is not merely some one thing among others but the precious pearl of the truth.[10]

Creation is not simply a theoretical question but provides a compass and direction for our lives. We cannot conceal our faith in creation:

> We *may* not conceal it, for only if it is true that the universe comes from freedom, love, and reason, and that these are the real underlying powers, can we trust one another, go forward into the future, and love as human beings. God is the Lord of all things because he is their creator, and only therefore can we pray to him. For this means that freedom and love are not ineffectual ideas but rather that they are sustaining forces of reality.[11]

Knowing that the universe comes from intelligence, freedom, and the beauty that is identical with love "gives us the courage to keep on living, and it empowers us, comforted thereby, to take upon ourselves the adventure of life".[12] We can know that it is truly a gift to be human only when we realize that we are not products of chance but that there is Someone who freely produced us out of love.[13]

The creation account in Genesis speaks of God creating the world in six days and resting on the seventh (see Gen 2:2–3). This points to a deeper truth: creation is oriented

---

[10] See Joseph Ratzinger, *Der Gott Jesu Christi: Betrachtungen über den Dreieinigen Gott* (Munich: Kösel, 2006), pp. 54–73, especially pp. 55–56.

[11] Ratzinger, *In the Beginning*, p. 18.

[12] Ibid., p. 25.

[13] See ibid., pp. 53–54, 56–57.

toward the Sabbath, which is the sign of the covenant between God and man. Creation is directed toward worship, which is the true center of our lives. This is a truth that was known, however vaguely, in all civilizations. However, this idea was often misinterpreted to mean that in worship man gives something to the gods of which they stand in need. The possibility lies open for manipulation, where man believes that the gods need him and he can therefore exploit them.

In the Bible, the notion that the universe exists for worship had to be purified. This was done by reference to the Sabbath, which is itself the summing up of the Torah, the law of Israel. Worship therefore has a moral aspect. It should be added that the Torah is an expression of Israel's history with God and thus of the covenant. The covenant itself is an expression of God's love, "of his 'yes' to the human being that he created, so that he could both love and receive love".[14] From this, we may conclude that God created the universe in order to enter into a history of love with mankind, so that love could exist outside of himself. Not only that, but he created the world in order to become man, so that he could "pour out his love upon us" and invite us "to love him in return".[15]

On the Sabbath day, man, in the freedom of worship, shares in God's freedom, in his rest and in his peace. To celebrate the Sabbath means to celebrate the covenant, to return to the source and "to sweep away all the defilement that our work has brought with it".[16] It also means going forth into a new world in which there will no longer be slaves or masters but only free children of God. From the

[14] Ibid., p. 29.
[15] Ibid., p. 30.
[16] Ibid., p. 31.

weekly Sabbath came the notion of the sabbatical year, every seventh year, when men and the earth would rest (see Lev 25:1–7), and the jubilee year, every seven times seven years, when all debts would be remitted and all purchases and sales annulled (see Lev 25:8–17; 23–55).[17] Fields and houses that had been alienated were returned to their original owners. A religious reason was adduced for this: land cannot be sold absolutely, because it belongs to God. Similarly, defaulting debtors and Israelite slaves were set free, for they are the servants of God who brought them out of Egypt. The earth is received back from the creating hands of God and everyone is to begin anew.[18]

The Exile was a traumatic event for Israel, during which time the people wondered why God had punished them in such a way, taking away from them his land, his temple, and his worship. The sins of the people, though many, did not seem to provide sufficient reason for such inordinate punishment. The real reason lay deeper, and we find it at the very end of the Second Book of Chronicles:

> [Nebuchadnezzar] took into exile in Babylon those who had escaped from the sword, and they became servants to him and to his sons until the establishment of the kingdom of Persia, to fulfil the word of the LORD by the mouth of Jeremiah, until the land had enjoyed its sabbaths. All the days that it lay desolate it kept sabbath, to fulfil seventy years.[19]

According to Joseph Ratzinger, this means that "the people had rejected God's rest, its leisure, its worship, its peace,

---

[17] On these two institutions, see Roland de Vaux, *Ancient Israel: Its Life and Institutions* (London: Darton, Longman and Todd, 1961), pp. 173–77.

[18] See Ratzinger, *In the Beginning*, p. 31.

[19] 2 Chron 36:20–21; cf. Jer 25:8–13; 29:10.

and its freedom, and so they fell into the slavery of activity." [20] The people had rejected the God-given rhythm of freedom and leisure, thus departing from their likeness to God and doing damage to the earth. They had to be snatched from their obstinate attachment to their own work. God had to begin afresh in order to make them once again his own. All of this points to a fundamental truth: the worship of God, his freedom, and his rest must come first. Only in this way can man truly live. [21]

In *The Spirit of the Liturgy*, Ratzinger expands on these points, emphasizing the intimate connection between worship, law, and ethics. Referring to the Exodus from Egypt, he explains that its purpose was twofold: to reach the Promised Land and to offer true worship to God. Indeed, the land "is given to the people to be a place for the worship of the true God". [22] The land, considered in itself, is an indeterminate good; it only becomes a true good when it is the place where God reigns, that is, when it becomes a place where God's will is done and the right kind of human existence is developed.

At Sinai, Israel came to know the kind of sacrifice that God desires. God makes a covenant with Israel, which included the Ten Commandments and stipulated the form of worship Israel was to follow. Israel is to worship God through set forms of ritual or liturgy and, more importantly, by living in accordance with God's will. The very life of man becomes true worship when he lives righteously, but life only becomes real life when it receives its form from looking toward God. The liturgy exists in order

---

[20] Ratzinger, *In the Beginning*, p. 32.

[21] See ibid.

[22] Ratzinger, *The Spirit of the Liturgy* (San Francisco: Ignatius Press, 2000), p. 17.

to communicate this vision and to give life in such a way that glory is given to God.

Furthermore, Israel received instructions about worship and an all-embracing rule of law and life. Only thus could she become a people. In the Sinai covenant, worship, law, and ethics are inseparably interwoven. When the Church spread to the Gentiles, some unraveling was required to make room for a diversity of legal forms and political structures. In modern times, however, this necessary unraveling "led finally to the total secularization of the law and the exclusion of any God-ward perspective from the fashioning of the law".[23] However, law without a foundation in morality becomes injustice, and when law and morality do not originate in a God-ward perspective, they degrade man because they rob him of his highest measure and capacity. This apparent liberation "subjects him to the dictatorship of the ruling majority, to shifting human standards, which inevitably end up doing him violence".[24] Without God, man is belittled. For this reason, Ratzinger concludes, worship and law cannot be completely separated from each other: "God has a right to a response from man, to man himself, and where that right of God totally disappears, the order of law among men is dissolved, because there is no cornerstone to keep the whole structure together." [25]

What took place on Sinai gives meaning to Israel's taking of the land. Sinai gives Israel her "interior land". Israel "is constituted as a people through the covenant and the divine law it contains".[26] This, and this alone, is what makes the land a real gift. Sinai continues to be present in the

[23] Ibid., p. 18.
[24] Ibid., p. 19.
[25] Ibid.
[26] Ibid.

Promised Land. When the reality of Sinai is lost, the reality
of the land is also inwardly lost, until finally the people are
thrust into Exile (this was the insight of the Chronicler in
2 Chron 36). Mere possession of the land is not sufficient
for freedom, and when the loss of law becomes total, it can
even lead to the loss of the land itself. The foundation for
existence in the Promised Land, for life in community and
freedom, must be steadfast adherence to the law of God,
which organizes human affairs rightly as realities that come
from God and are meant to return to him.

Worship in its full sense goes beyond liturgy. It embraces
the ordering of the entirety of human life. Man offers true
worship to God when he recognizes himself as a creature
made for God's glory and lives by looking toward God.
Law and ethics do not hold together unless they are anchored
in the liturgical center and inspired by it: law is essential for
life in community and freedom, while worship, which is
the right way to relate to God, is essential for law and for
the right kind of human existence in the world. Worship,
says Ratzinger, "gives us a share in heaven's mode of existence, in the world of God, and allows light to fall from
that divine world into ours".[27] It anticipates a more perfect
life, giving the present life its true measure. Life without
such anticipation would be hollow and empty. Man cannot
make up this worship for himself. True liturgy implies that
God responds and it reveals how we can worship him; it
implies a real relationship with Another, who reveals himself to us and gives our existence a new direction.

True worship thus involves a right relationship with
God. This relationship is based in the first place on the fact
that man is created by God. According to the account in

[27] Ibid., p. 21.

Genesis 2, man is formed from the dust of the earth. This symbolic language contains a truth that is both humbling and consoling: humbling, because man is not God, but a limited creature, destined for death like all other living things; consoling, because the Genesis account teaches that man has been formed not by any demonic forces but from God's good earth.[28] Since all are formed from the one earth, the human race is one; there are not fundamentally different kinds of human beings. This is the basis for the Christian rejection of racism in all its forms. There is something more. God enters into the creation of man by breathing into his nostrils the breath of life (see Gen 2:7). The first creation account says this in a deeper way: man is created in God's image and likeness (see Gen 1:26–27). This means that every man is directly related to God: he is known, loved, and willed by God. Human life stands under God's special protection, for every man bears God's breath in himself and is created in God's image.

Man's condition as image ultimately means that he is capable of relationship with God, of thinking about him and praying to him. Christ is the second and final Adam and the image of God in the fullest sense (see 1 Cor 15:44–48; Col 1:15). Hence, in Christ alone appears the complete answer to the question concerning what man is.[29] Man becomes fully himself by relating to Christ, dying with him in order to rise with him. Consequently, we must always see in other people "persons with whom we shall one day share God's joy ... who are called, together with us, to be members of the Body of Christ, with whom we shall one day sit at table with Abraham, Isaac, and Jacob, and with

[28] See Ratzinger, *In the Beginning*, pp. 42–43.

[29] See ibid., pp. 48–49, 57–58; also Pope John Paul II, *Redemptor Hominis*, March 4, 1979, no. 10.

Christ himself".[30] In all of this, we discover the deepest reason for the inviolability of human dignity.

When man is no longer perceived in this way, then he comes to be seen in a merely utilitarian fashion and his dignity is at serious risk of being trampled upon by the resulting barbarity. This is the great danger of our modern technological age. Where reason is limited to what can be corroborated by experiment or computation, the ethical and the sacred no longer count for anything. When this happens, anything that is scientifically possible appears legitimate and the individual is in serious danger of being crushed. Man is not God but a creature, made in God's image, dependent on him, and destined to share eternal life with him. Recognition of this truth is vital in order to protect human dignity and set limits on what man can do with his technological advances.[31] Man's dependence on God is in no way degrading, for this dependence is really an expression of love. Love, as we saw earlier, essentially takes the form of saying: "I want you to be." Hence, love is creative: it constitutes the self as self and sets it free. God's love transforms dependence into freedom: we may freely choose to accept it as the foundation for authentic human existence or reject it, thereby destroying ourselves.[32]

Man's creaturely condition sets the standard for his activity in the world. However, creation sets in motion a story of love and freedom. This entails a risk: "As the arena of love [the world] is also the playground of freedom and also incurs the risk of evil."[33] Man is created with freedom, which implies that he is capable of sinning. At the very

---

[30] Ratzinger, *In the Beginning*, p. 49.

[31] See ibid., pp. 43–47.

[32] See ibid., pp. 98–99.

[33] Ratzinger, *Introduction to Christianity*, 2nd ed., p. 160.

heart of sin is the refusal to accept one's creatureliness, and
the standards and limitations implicit in it. This is the profound meaning behind the temptation and sin of the first
parents in Genesis 3. The first temptation is to doubt God's
covenant and the context for living it, namely, the community of faith, prayer, and the commandments.[34] It is all
too easy to believe or convince others that God's covenant
is not a gift, but an imposition, robbing man of what is
most precious in life and denying him his freedom. Once
man doubts the covenant and frees himself from the limitations imposed by his created condition, the good and the
moral disappear and the belief takes over that one *may* do
whatever one *can* do. This opposition to the truth, as history teaches, leads to self-deception and self-destruction and
produces the worst horrors of which man is capable:

> [Those] who consider dependence on the highest love as
> slavery and who try to deny the truth about themselves,
> which is their creatureliness, do not free themselves; they
> destroy truth and love. They do not make themselves gods,
> which in fact they cannot do, but rather caricatures, pseudo-
> gods, slaves of their own abilities, which then drag them
> down.[35]

Sin, in its denial of truth and love, is the enemy of joy,
for there can be no joy that is not based on truth and
love. The sinner appears to be in a hopeless condition: his
rejection of the truth is self-destructive and leads to despair.
Sin destroys man's fundamental relationships with God and
with others. It also alters and damages the world. Since
the network of human relationships was damaged from the
very beginning, on account of the sin of the first parents,

[34] See Ratzinger, *In the Beginning*, pp. 66–67.
[35] Ibid., pp. 70–71.

everyone "enters into a world that is marked by relational damage".[36] This is the fundamental truth underlying the doctrine of original sin. Because of it, it is clear that man alone cannot save himself: "We can only be saved—that is, be free and true—when we stop wanting to be God and when we renounce the madness of autonomy and self-sufficiency." [37] Our salvation requires a healing of relationships. Since the damage has been done in this regard at the level of our creatureliness, we can be saved only by the Creator himself: "Only being loved is being saved, and only God's love can purify damaged love and radically re-establish the network of relationships that have suffered from alienation." [38]

Into this situation comes Jesus Christ, the divine Son who takes on human flesh, entering into our creaturely limitations, in order to restore us to ourselves. His fundamental message of salvation, the "glad tidings", is synthesized at the beginning of St. Mark's Gospel: "The time is fulfilled, and the kingdom of God is at hand; repent [*metanoeite*], and believe in the gospel" (1:15). Our salvation requires us to acknowledge our sinfulness, do penance, and become other than we are.[39]

Jesus is the new and final Adam, who goes Adam's route in reverse. He is the true image of God (see Phil 2:6). In his case, the similarity lies in the fact that he is the Son and is therefore completely relational. He does not hold graspingly to his authority but becomes completely dependent, like a slave (see Phil 2:6–7). By taking the route of love rather than that of power, "he can descend into the depths

[36] Ibid., p. 73.
[37] Ibid.
[38] Ibid., p. 74.
[39] See ibid., p. 61.

of Adam's lie, into the depths of death, and there raise up truth and life." [40] In Christ, the new Adam, mankind begins anew. The Son, who is by nature relationship and relatedness, repairs the damage to our relationships. On the Cross, his open arms invite us into true relationship. From the Cross, the tree of life, the word of obedience and redeeming love comes forth, not the word of temptation. Jesus' obedience, which is the standard of creatureliness, is the context for our freedom. Dependence on God, which creatureliness implies, is not an imposition but the condition for true freedom and true joy.

[40] Ibid., pp. 75–76.

Chapter VI

JESUS CHRIST, BEARER OF JOY

Inspired by the tradition linking Cologne with the relics of the Magi, the celebration in August 2005 of World Youth Day had as its principal theme the Gospel text: "We . . . have come to worship him" (Mt 2:2). In his opening address to the young people gathered on the banks of the Rhine, Pope Benedict XVI referred to the Magi's search for the infant king of the Jews, seeing it as emblematic of the perennial human yearning for the response capable of satisfying the heart's deepest desires. The frail body of a child, containing the One whom the entire world cannot contain, proved to be the goal of the Magi's quest. Christ continues today to provide the answer to the questions of meaning, salvation, and ultimate happiness that we all ask. Stressing that only Jesus Christ gives the fullness of life to mankind, the Holy Father encouraged those present to commit themselves to Christ's service: the "encounter with Jesus Christ", he said, "will allow you to experience in your hearts the joy of his living and life-giving presence and enable you to bear witness to it before others." [1]

[1] Benedict XVI, Address at the celebration welcoming the young people, August 18, 2005, in Benedict XVI, *God's Revolution: World Youth Day and Other Cologne Talks* (San Francisco: Ignatius Press, 2006), p. 39.

Later, outside Cologne's immense Gothic cathedral, the Pope continued his Christ-centered catechesis with a prayer:

> Through you, may other young people everywhere come to recognize in Christ the true answer to their deepest aspirations, and may they open their hearts to receive the Word of God Incarnate, who died and rose so that God might dwell among us and give us the truth, love and joy for which we are all yearning.[2]

At the vigil and concluding Mass celebrated in Marienfeld, Pope Benedict's conviction that Jesus Christ is the bearer of true joy re-emerged in all its force. Joy arises from knowing the true face of God and the ultimate meaning of life, which Christ reveals. It flows from coming into contact with God's goodness and love, made known by Christ, especially through his death and Resurrection. By adoring God and entering into his service, we experience true joy and happiness. This joy, as the Pope emphasized, is meant to be shared: "Anyone who has discovered Christ must lead others to him. A great joy cannot be kept to oneself. It has to be passed on."[3]

At the Cologne celebrations, Pope Benedict revealed something of his own personal faith and spirituality: both are deeply rooted in friendship with Christ.[4] The mystery of Christ, his saving work, and our vocation to enter into this mystery are at the heart of the Pope's teaching. This focus emerges clearly in the theological and spiritual writings of

[2] Benedict XVI, Address at Cologne Cathedral, August 18, 2005, in ibid., p. 44.

[3] Benedict XVI, Homily at the concluding Mass of World Youth Day, August 21, 2005, in ibid., p. 60.

[4] On this theme, see Philippe Raguis, "Une foi profondément enracinée dans le Christ", in *Kephas* 17 (2006): 35–44.

Joseph Ratzinger, which emphasize the inseparability of the person and work of Jesus Christ as the key to a balanced understanding of the central mysteries of Christ's Incarnation and work of redemption.[5]

Through appeal to the notion of person as relatedness and the Pauline Christology of the final Adam, Joseph Ratzinger synthesizes the two basic approaches to the mystery of Jesus Christ, based respectively on the Incarnation and the Cross. Ratzinger also draws attention to the significance of Christ's prayer as the basis for the early Church's understanding of his relation of sonship to the Father and his saving work. Christ's manner of praying also sheds light on the meaning of salvation, freedom, and liberation. Through his death and Resurrection, Christ brings about our salvation. While St. Anselm's notion of satisfaction proved highly influential in theological reflection on Christ's saving work, Ratzinger favors a theory of representation or substitution (*Stellvertretung*), which he sees as closer to the biblical evidence, and he describes the saving meaning of Jesus' death in terms of his loving self-surrender to the Father.

1. Approaches to the mystery of Jesus Christ

From earliest times, there have been two main approaches to the mystery of Jesus Christ: one focusing on the Incarnation,

[5] Joseph Ratzinger has written much in the area of Christology, particularly in *Introduction to Christianity*, 2nd ed. (San Francisco: Ignatius Press, 2004), *The God of Jesus Christ: Meditations on God in the Trinity* (Chicago Franciscan Herald Press, 1978), *Journey towards Easter: Retreat given in the Vatican in the presence of Pope John Paul II* (Slough: St Paul's Publications, 1987), *Behold the Pierced One: An Approach to a Spiritual Christology* (San Francisco: Ignatius Press, 1986), *On the Way to Jesus Christ* (San Francisco: Ignatius Press, 2005), and *Jesus of Nazareth: From the Baptism in the Jordan to the Transfiguration* (New York: Doubleday, 2007).

the other on the Cross. The former centers on the person
of Jesus Christ, and on the fact that here a man is God
and that God is man. In this approach, the interlocking of
God and man "appears as the truly decisive, redemptive
factor, as the real future of man, on which all lines must
finally converge".[6] The latter speaks of the event of the
Cross and explores its significance, emphasizing the victory of Christ over sin and death, and its redemptive meaning for mankind.

A correct understanding of the mystery of Christ, inso-
far as that is possible to our limited minds, must embrace
both approaches. On the one hand, a theology of the Incarnation separated from the theology of the Cross could easily become an abstract speculation on the unity and
distinction of the two natures in Christ, shedding little light
on what it ultimately means to be human. Alternatively,
even when the connection between the ontological constitution of Christ and the mystery of human existence is
emphasized, there is still a risk of not paying sufficient heed
to the reality of sin, thus producing too optimistic a theology of man's progression to convergence with God. On
the other hand, a theology of the Cross separated from the
theology of the Incarnation could become an antiworld interpretation of Christianity and could fail to show how Christ's
being, with all that it reveals about what man truly is, sheds
light on the meaning of his saving work. There are undeniable polarities in the two approaches, but these must be
held in order for one approach to correct and complement
the other and so arrive at a better understanding of the
whole.[7]

[6] Ratzinger, *Introduction to Christianity*, 2nd ed., p. 229.
[7] See ibid., pp. 228–31.

An adequate grasp of the mystery of Christ requires paying due attention to the unity of his person and saving work. Ratzinger articulates this by appeal to the category of relatedness:

The *being* of Christ ("Incarnation" theology!) is *actualitas*, stepping beyond oneself, the exodus of going out from self; it is not a being that rests in itself, but the act of being sent, of being son, of serving. Conversely, this "doing" is not just "doing" but "being"; it reaches down into the depths of being and coincides with it. This being is exodus, transformation. So at this point a properly understood Christology of being and of the Incarnation must pass over into the theology of the Cross and become one with it; conversely, a theology of the Cross developed to its full extent must become a Christology of Son and being.[8]

Ratzinger's approach to the mystery of Christ is heavily influenced by his understanding of person in terms of relatedness (being "from" and being "for"), and by St. Paul's teaching that Jesus is the "last Adam" (see 1 Cor 15:45) or the exemplary man, who reveals what the enigma of the human person truly is, by bringing the idea of man to fulfillment and making perfectly clear the direction in which he is ultimately tending.[9] Applying the idea, developed in connection with the discussion on the Trinity, that man comes to himself only by moving away from himself toward the other, Ratzinger says:

Because [Christ] is the exemplary, the authoritative man, he oversteps the bounds of humanity; only thus and only thereby is he the truly exemplary man. For man is the more

[8] Ibid., p. 230 (translation slightly modified).
[9] See ibid., p. 234; also Joseph Ratzinger, "Concerning the Notion of Person in Theology", in *Communio* (America ed.) 17 (1990): 450.

himself the more he is with the "other". He only comes *to* himself by moving away *from* himself. Only through "the other" and through "being" with "the other" does he come to himself.[10]

But man is not intended for just any other, who could cause him to be lost. He is intended for *the* other, for the truly other who is God:

> Accordingly, he is completely himself when he has ceased to exist for himself, to shut himself off in himself, and to assert himself, when in fact he is pure openness to God. To put it again in different terms: man comes to himself by moving out beyond himself. Jesus Christ, though, is the one who has moved right out beyond himself and, *thus*, the man who has truly come to himself.[11]

Jesus Christ is fully man, indeed, he is the fullness of what it means to be human. As Ratzinger explains, it is openness to the whole, to the infinite, that makes man complete: "Man is man by reaching out infinitely beyond himself, and he is consequently more of a man the less enclosed he is in himself, the less 'limited' he is."[12] Hence, Jesus is most fully man, the true man, because he not only has contact with Infinite Being, but is one with him.

This being the case, Christ's existence concerns all mankind. In this lies the significance of the theology of the final Adam. "Adam" is a corporate name, which the Bible uses to express the unity of the whole creature "man". By referring to Christ as Adam, St. Paul implies that he is to gather the whole creature "Adam" in himself. His existence is one

[10] Ratzinger, *Introduction to Christianity*, 2nd ed., p. 234.
[11] Ibid., pp. 234–35 (translation slightly modified).
[12] Ibid., p. 235.

that is to draw to itself all of mankind (cf. Jn 12:32), into the unity of the "body of Christ".[13]

For St. John, the Cross of Christ brings scattered mankind together in unity. The Crucifixion is a process of opening, in which separated individuals who exist only for themselves, like monads, are drawn together into the embrace of Christ's open and outstretched arms. This being so, Christ as the man to come is not man for himself but essentially man for others; it is his essential openness that makes him the man for the future. In order to make genuine progress, we must leave behind the man of the past, the man who exists only for himself. Ratzinger's understanding of the person as relatedness comes out very strongly here: "The future of man", he says, "lies in 'being for'." It is clear then that Christ's sonship and the doctrine of the three Persons in God are to be understood in terms of "dynamic, 'actual' existence, which is essentially openness in the movement between 'from' and 'for'".[14]

Christ is the completely open man, in whom the dividing walls of existence are torn down; he is entirely "transition" or "Passover", as St. John depicts him in the scene of his pierced side, from which blood and water flow (see Jn 19:34). This scene is the climax not only of the Crucifixion account but of the whole story of Jesus. With the piercing of his side, his existence is completely open; "now he is entirely 'for'; now he is truly no longer a single individual but 'Adam', from whose side Eve, a new mankind, is formed." [15] The blood and water point to the basic Christian sacraments of baptism and the Eucharist, and through

---

[13] See ibid., p. 236.
[14] Ibid., p. 240.
[15] Ibid., p. 241.

them to the Church as the sign of the new community of
men and women. The man who exists for others, who
opens up a new beginning for them, is sacrificed man.
The future of man hangs on the Cross: his redemption is
the Cross. Man's salvation, his coming to himself, involves
letting the walls of his existence be broken down, by looking on the One who has been pierced (see Jn 19:37) and
by following him.

Christianity, which in the doctrine of creation recognizes the primacy of the Logos, the creative meaning as
beginning and origin, also acknowledges the Logos as the
end, the future, the coming one. Hence, it is not just a
looking back to what happened in the past, or an outlook
on the eternal, but is also, above all, a looking forward in
hope. It is not utopianism, for hope's goal is not man's own
product. This hope is sure because of (1) the breakthrough
that occurred in the past, (2) the present of the eternal,
which makes divided time like unity, and (3) the looking
forward to him who is to come, in whom God and the
world will touch each other. Faith advances to meet the
one who is coming, but, in Christ, the countenance of
the one who is to come is already revealed: he "is the man
who can embrace all men because he has lost himself and
them to God".[16]

2. The prayer of Jesus

To understand better what has been said up to now, it will
prove instructive to examine how the Church's belief regarding the person of Christ developed from her reflection on
his relationship with God, particularly as expressed in his

[16] Ibid., pp. 242–43.

prayer.[17] Amid the plethora of titles applied to him in early times (Prophet, Priest, Messiah, Lord, and so forth), the title of "Son" turned out to be the most satisfactory, as it comprises and interprets all the others.[18] This title corresponds most strictly to what is central to the historical figure of Jesus. The entire Gospel testimony is unanimous in holding that his words and deeds flowed from his most intimate communion with the Father, expressed in frequent and prolonged prayer.

St. Luke, in particular, shows how the essential events of Jesus' activity, such as the call of the Twelve, in which the Church first began to take shape, and the Transfiguration, proceeded from the core of his personality: his dialogue with the Father. Peter's confession of faith occurs when the disciples begin to share in the prayer of Jesus; he was able to grasp and express who Jesus is from seeing him praying (see Lk 9:18–20). Luke makes it clear that the Christian confession of faith "comes from participating in the prayer of Jesus, from being drawn into his prayer and being privileged to behold it"; in short, the Church "arises out of participation in the prayer of Jesus".[19]

Entering into the prayer of Jesus through our own prayer is the basic precondition for coming to know him as he is in his intimate relationship with the Father. All knowledge involves a certain unity of the knower and the known, without suppressing their distinction. Accordingly, in the case

[17] On this theme, see especially ibid., pp. 223–28; Ratzinger, *Behold the Pierced One*, pp. 13–46; Ratzinger, *Journey towards Easter*, pp. 78–91. The immediate relationship of Jesus to the Father, which is the true center of his personality, is also central to the argument of *Jesus of Nazareth*.

[18] See Ratzinger, *Behold the Pierced One*, pp. 16–17.

[19] Ibid., p. 19; cf. ibid., pp. 25–27; also Ratzinger, *Jesus of Nazareth*, pp. 290–91.

of the mind and where persons are concerned, knowledge requires a certain degree of empathy by which we enter, so to speak, into the intellectual reality or person concerned, to become one with it and thus to understand. Just as we can acquire philosophy only by engaging in philosophical thinking, so too we can understand religion only by taking part in it, especially through the fundamental religious act that is prayer. Christian prayer is an act of self-surrender by which we enter into the body of Christ; it is an act of love. Relationship with God through prayer, through love, is the prerequisite for understanding him. The one who prays begins to see; praying and seeing go together, for "love is the faculty of seeing." As Ratzinger says, all real progress in theological understanding "has its origin in the eye of love and in its faculty of beholding".[20]

Sharing in Christ's prayer enables us to understand him as the Son; indeed, the Christology expressed by the title "Son" is essentially a theology of prayer, a concentration of the witnesses' experience with the person of Jesus.[21] The relationship of sonship is expressed elsewhere in the Gospels by Jesus' use of the Aramaic word "Abba" to address the Father in a particularly familiar and intimate way (see Mk 14:36) and in his description of himself as Son, particularly in St. John's Gospel, where it is linked with the expression "I am", which points to the divine being of Christ.[22] The title "Son" "draws us into that intimacy which Jesus reserved for those who were his friends".[23] It conveys the total relatedness of his

[20] Ratzinger, *Behold the Pierced One*, p. 27.

[21] See Ratzinger, *Journey towards Easter*, p. 84; on what follows, see also Ratzinger, *Jesus of Nazareth*, pp. 339–45.

[22] On this, see Ratzinger, *Introduction to Christianity*, 2nd ed., pp. 223–28, 276.

[23] Ratzinger, *Behold the Pierced One*, p. 22.

existence, his being "from" and "for" the Father. In this regard, the title "Son" coincides with the designations "Word" and "the one sent". John's Son-Christology once again emphasizes the identity of Jesus' work and being: he keeps nothing back for himself but gives himself completely in his work. Jesus' entire being is service, and, as such, it is sonship.[24]

Sharing in Christ's prayer has another consequence: it is the place where man's true liberation takes place. To talk about Christ is to talk about salvation, about man's definitive liberation. But what is freedom? Freedom must be connected with truth; otherwise, it is falsehood, deception, and slavery. At heart, man knows that his freedom lies in becoming like God. Everything else fails to satiate his desire. How is this to be achieved? As the Genesis account of the fall teaches us, the temptation constantly besieging man is to become like God, not with divine help, but by rejecting God and setting out to do so on his own (cf. Gen 3:5). The problem of human liberation can in fact be solved only by seeing it in connection with the question of the truth of man's own being and, ultimately, with the question of God.

The discussion on Christ's prayer is concerned not only with who he is, but also with man, his being and his freedom. By entering into this prayer, man touches his own truth and becomes true himself:

> The question of Jesus' filial relation to the Father gets to the very root of the question of man's freedom and liberation, and unless this is done everything else is futile. Any liberation of man which does not enable him to become divine betrays man, betrays his boundless yearning.[25]

[24] See Ratzinger, *Introduction to Christianity*, 2nd ed., p. 226.
[25] Ratzinger, *Behold the Pierced One*, p. 35; cf. Ratzinger, *Journey towards Easter*, p. 87.

In this connection, we come to see how the early Church councils shed light not only on the person of Christ but also on the meaning of man and his freedom. The core of the Christological teaching of these councils consists in the statement that "Jesus is the true Son of God, of the same essence as the Father and, through the Incarnation, equally of the same essence as us."[26] This definition provides an interpretation in technical language of the life and death of Jesus, which were preordained from the Son's primal conversation with the Father.[27] In 325 the First Council of Nicaea declared that the Son is of the same substance as the Father and, by using the newly coined term *homoousios*, made it clear that the New Testament name is to be understood not metaphorically but in all its literal truth.[28]

This teaching, says Ratzinger, is reason for joy, since, in contrast to the Arian emphasis on the utter otherness of God, which would imply that God is too great to interest himself in the world or come close to us in history, it indicates that God can and does intervene in the world, and that he has truly become man in Jesus Christ.[29] In Jesus, God is no longer hidden. He touches man and allows us to touch him in the person of him who *is* the Son. This is the truth on which we can live and die.[30]

In his discussion on the significance of the Third Council of Constantinople (680–681), Ratzinger develops the theme of how our freedom is realized through its insertion

[26] Ratzinger, *Behold the Pierced One*, p. 32.

[27] See ibid.; also Ratzinger, *Journey towards Easter*, p. 85.

[28] See Ratzinger, *Behold the Pierced One*, p. 36; also Ratzinger, *Journey towards Easter*, pp. 87–88; Ratzinger, *Jesus of Nazareth*, p. 320.

[29] See Ratzinger, *Der Gott Jesu Christi: Betrachtungen über den Dreieinigen Gott* (Munich: Kösel, 2006), pp. 143–44.

[30] See Ratzinger, *Behold the Pierced One*, p. 36; Ratzinger, *Journey towards Easter*, p. 88.

into Christ's prayer.[31] Over two centuries earlier, the Council of Chalcedon (451) had sought to respond to the Monophysite heresy of Eutyches by teaching that "one and the same Christ, Lord and only-begotten Son, is to be acknowledged in two natures without confusion, change, division or separation".[32] The distinction between the two natures was not abolished by their union. Instead, the character proper to each of the natures was preserved as they came together in one person (*prosōpon*) and one hypostasis. The definition of Chalcedon did not win universal acceptance, and heated discussion on the person and natures of Christ continued unabated in that Council's aftermath.

At the Third Council of Constantinople, the Chalcedonian formula was explored in its implications for Christ's will and activity. Against the Monothelite and Monoenergist views that, while Christ has both human and divine natures, he does not have a genuine human will (*thelēma*) or activity (*energeia*), the Council affirmed that the unity of God and man in the person of Christ involves no amputation or lessening of his human nature. In conjoining himself to man, God does not diminish man but brings him for the first time to his real fullness.

The Council also avoids dualistic or parallel understandings of the two natures, such as had always seemed necessary to safeguard Christ's human freedom. When human will is taken up into the will of God, it is not destroyed; indeed, only then does genuine freedom come into its own. Christ's human will is not absorbed into the divine will but follows it, becoming one with it, not in a natural way but along the path of freedom. The unity of wills takes place not at the

---

[31] On this, see Ratzinger, *Behold the Pierced One*, pp. 37–42.
[32] Council of Chalcedon, Symbol of Faith (DS 302).

level of natures but in the realm of the person that is the
realm of freedom. It is a form of unity created by love, which
is higher and more interior than a merely natural unity.

This free unity corresponds to the highest unity there is,
namely, the unity of the Blessed Trinity. In this regard, the
Council quotes the words of Jesus: "I have come down from
heaven, not to do my own will, but the will of him who
sent me" (Jn 6:38). It is the divine Logos who is speaking,
and he is speaking of the human will of the man Jesus as his
will, the will of the Logos. By quoting this text, the Council
emphasizes the unity of subject in Christ: there are not two
"I"s in him, but only one. His human will is completely one
with the will of the Logos, a pure Yes to the Father's will.

Some years earlier, the great monk-theologian Maximus
the Confessor (580–662) had worked out the central distinction that is fundamental to the Council's teaching.[33] At
the level of nature, there exists a natural will (*thelēma phusikon*);
this exists separately in Christ's divinity and humanity. However, at the level of person, there is only a single will (*thelēma
gnōmikon*). To illustrate this, Maximus refers to Jesus' prayer
in the Garden. In this scene, it is as if we were actually looking in on the inner life of the Word-made-man in his intimate and unique relation to the Father. His words "not what
I will, but what you will" (Mk 14:36) are the measure and
model of all real prayer. His human will assimilates itself to
the will of the Son. In this prayer, we see how the "I" is
completely subordinate to the "Thou" in its self-giving and
self-expropriation to the "Thou". It expresses the very essence
of him who is pure relation and pure act. When the "I"

[33] On this, see François-Marie Léthel, *Théologie de l'agonie du Christ: La
liberté humaine du Fils de Dieu et son importance sotériologique mises en lumière par
Saint Maxime Confesseur* (Paris: Beauchesne, 1979).

gives itself to the "Thou" in this way, there is freedom, because this involves the reception of the "form of God".[34]

To put it in another way, the Logos so humbles himself that he assumes a man's will as his own and addresses the Father with the "I" of this human being: "He transfers his own I to this man and thus transforms human speech into the eternal Word, into his blessed 'Yes, Father'."[35] In this way, by imparting his own identity to this human being, he liberates him, redeems him, and makes him God. We can now better understand the real meaning of "God has become man": "The Son transforms the anguish of a man into his own filial obedience, the speech of the servant into the Word who is the Son."[36]

In this way, we are able to grasp our own path to liberation, our sharing in the freedom of the Son. Through the unity of wills, the greatest possible change has taken place in man, the only change that meets his desire: he has become divine. The prayer that enters into the prayer of Jesus may then be described as a "laboratory of freedom".[37] Here and nowhere else takes place that radical change in man of which we stand in need, so that the world may become a better place. This is because it is only along this path that conscience attains its fundamental soundness and its unshakeable power, and only from such a conscience can there come that ordering of human affairs which corresponds to human dignity and protects it.[38]

---

[34] See Ratzinger, *Behold the Pierced One*, p. 41; Ratzinger, *Journey towards Easter*, p. 90.

[35] Ratzinger, *Behold the Pierced One*, p. 41.

[36] Ibid.

[37] Ibid., p. 42.

[38] Conscience is a central theme in Ratzinger's writings. For a presentation of his teaching on this topic, see especially D. Vincent Twomey, *Pope*

Christ's prayer sheds light on his saving work on the Cross; in it, we discover the clue linking his person with his deeds and sufferings. Although they differ in detail, the four evangelists agree that Jesus died praying, thus making his death an act of prayer and worship. His last words expressed his devotion to his Father, and his death cry was addressed to no one but the Father, since "it was of his innermost essence to be in a dialogue relationship with the Father." [39]

Christ's death is what opens for us the path of life, and his Resurrection causes the most profound joy. In *The God of Jesus Christ* (*Der Gott Jesu Christi*) and again in *Journey towards Easter*, Ratzinger reflects on Christ's sharing in the human experience of the condition of death. [40] In Christ's case, this is quite mysterious. On the one hand, he truly died. Death put an end to his earthly human existence, causing the separation of his soul from his body, according to the necessary order of nature. On the other, both body and soul remained united to his divine person and his body was preserved from corruption. [41] In his meditation on Christ's death, Ratzinger stresses the solidarity of Christ with all the dead and therefore focuses on the significance of the separation in death of Christ's soul from his body.

Benedict XVI: The Conscience of Our Age. A Theological Portrait (San Francisco: Ignatius Press, 2007); for a shorter account, see D. Vincent Twomey, "La conscience chez le Pape Benoît XVI", in *Kephas* 17 (2006): 89–100.

[39] Ratzinger, *Behold the Pierced One*, p. 22; cf. Ratzinger, *Journey towards Easter*, pp. 102–10.

[40] See Ratzinger, *Der Gott Jesu Christi*, pp. 133–36; Ratzinger, *Journey towards Easter*, pp 108–10. For Ratzinger's theology of death, see his *Eschatology: Death and Eternal Life* (Washington, D.C.: Catholic University of America Press, 1988), pp. 69–103.

[41] See *Catechism of the Catholic Church*, nos. 624–30.

As Ratzinger explains, from the biological perspective, to be human means having to die. In this sense, death is both natural and necessary. However, man also has a spiritual dimension that aspires to eternity and, from this point of view, to die is not natural but illogical, "because it means expulsion from the sphere of loving, destruction of that connecting element which is the desire of eternity".[42] The contradiction inherent in human death reaches its culmination in Jesus Christ. For him, who lived fully in communion and in dialogue with the Father, death in its absolute solitariness is incomprehensible. Yet, in order to bring God's saving plan to fulfillment, death has a specific necessity for him. His special relationship with the Father was, in fact, the cause of his own people's incomprehension and, consequently, of his solitude during his earthly life. His death is "the final act consequent on this incomprehension, the relegation of what is misunderstood to a zone of silence".[43]

Death, then, is both a biological and a spiritual happening. While the divine Person of the Son, being eternal, continues to relate to the Father, Ratzinger argues that the destruction of the body, the instrument of human communication, causes an interruption in Christ's dialogue (as man) with his heavenly Father:

> When the human instrument comes to fall away, the spiritual action which is founded on it also disappears, temporarily. Thus something more is shattered here than in any ordinary death. There is an interruption of that dialogue which in reality is the axis of the whole world.[44]

[42] Ratzinger, *Journey towards Easter*, p. 108.
[43] Ibid., p. 109.
[44] Ibid.

The opening verse of Psalm 22, "My God, my God, why have you forsaken me?" uttered by Jesus on the Cross (Mt 27:46; Mk 15:34), gives some indication of the abyssal depths of this process. However, his dialogue with the Father, which in his earthly life sets him apart as having a unique relationship with the Father, does not end in death but points forward to his rising from the dead. While Psalm 22 begins with a description of the atrocious sufferings of the just man, it concludes on a confident note: the just man will be vindicated and will sing God's praises in the liturgical assembly.

The Resurrection of Jesus Christ, the just man par excellence, is the central truth of the Christian faith. His victory over death is the basis for our joy. His confident prayer has been answered: God raises him to new life, placing his human existence safely within the Trinitarian dialogue of eternal love. Jesus is man today and remains so forever. Through him, human existence has penetrated into the very being of God, and so we too are in God. God is thus both the "Totally Other" and the "Non-Other". As Ratzinger explains, it is Jesus Christ who teaches us to call God "Father"; when we do, we do so with Christ and in God himself. Man's hope, Christian joy, and the gospel itself lie in this: Christ is man today. In him, God has truly become Not-Other. Man, then, may no longer be considered absurd, he is not deprived of consolation, and so we can rejoice. God loves us so much that his love became and remains flesh. Such a joy, Ratzinger insists, should inspire and strengthen us to communicate God's love to others also, so that they too can gladden themselves with the light that has come to us and that, in the depth of the world's night, is a harbinger of the day.[45]

[45] See ibid., pp. 109–10.

3. The death and Resurrection of Jesus

Various theories have been put forward to explain the role
played by Christ's death in bringing about our salvation.[46]
Some are clearly biblical in origin while others, though pos-
sessing a biblical foundation, were developed by subsequent
theological reflection. As no one theory explains all aspects
of this mystery, the *Catechism of the Catholic Church* appeals
to a number of them in its section on Christ's death, while
placing the emphasis on God's initiative and Christ's loving
response.[47] Christ's death is the sacrifice that brings about
the definitive redemption of man, restoring him to communion with God by reconciling him to God, through the
blood of the covenant that was poured out for the forgiveness of sins (see Mt 26:28; 1 Cor 11:25). The *Catechism*
emphasizes that Christ offered his life to the Father in freedom and love in reparation for our disobedience. Christ's
love "to the end" (Jn 13:1) confers on his sacrifice its value
as redemption and reparation, atonement and satisfaction.
He substituted his obedience for our disobedience:

> "For as by one man's disobedience many were made sinners,
> so by one man's obedience many will be made righteous"
> (Rom 5:19). By his obedience unto death, Jesus accom-
> plished the substitution of the suffering Servant, who "makes
> himself an *offering for sin*," when "he bore the sins of many,"
> and who "shall make many to be accounted righteous," for
> "he shall bear their iniquities" (Is 53:10–12). Jesus atoned
> for our faults and made satisfaction for our sins to the Father.[48]

[46] For a discussion of these theories, see Bernard Sesboüé, *Jésus-Christ,
l'unique médiateur*, 2 vols. (Paris: Desclée, 1988, 1991), especially vol. 1.

[47] See *Catechism of the Catholic Church*, nos. 599–617.

[48] Ibid., no. 615. On atonement and satisfaction, see Council of Trent,
Decree on Justification, c. 7 (DS 1529).

In traditional Catholic theology, St. Anselm's theory of satisfaction played a major part in trying to explain why Jesus' death on the Cross was necessary for our salvation. According to this theory, only Christ, being both God and man, could make the necessary infinite reparation for the infinite offense caused to God by man's sin, and in this way restore the order of justice that had been violated.[49] While Joseph Ratzinger believes that the theory has merits, particularly in its emphasis on the fact that we live not only directly from God, but also from one another, and, in the final analysis, from the One who lived for all, he is of the view that this "logical divine-*cum*-human system" could lead to a distortion of perspectives and make the image of God appear in a sinister light.[50]

While not excluding other approaches, Ratzinger's own preferred explanation is in terms of a theory of representation or substitution (*Stellvertretung*), according to which Christ stands in our place, making the definitive self-offering of love to God that man by himself is powerless to make.[51] This explanation should not be seen in isolation but in relation to what has been said earlier about the unity of Christ's person and work, according to which he is the one whose whole existence is to be for others, about Christ as the final Adam who unites all humanity in himself, leading it back to God, and about created freedom, which is fully realized when it is taken up into the freedom of Christ, and appropriates the salvation that he offers.

---

[49] For a brief account of this theory, see Ratzinger, *Introduction to Christianity*, 2nd ed., pp. 231–33.

[50] Ibid., p. 233; cf. ibid., p. 281.

[51] See Joseph Ratzinger, "Stellvertretung", in *Handbuch Theologischer Grundbegriffe*, ed. Heinrich Fries, vol. 2 (Munich: Kösel, 1963), pp. 566–75; Ratzinger, *Introduction to Christianity*, 2nd ed., pp. 281–93.

Ratzinger holds that the Bible, in fact, does not see the Cross as part of a mechanism of injured right, but as the expression of the radical nature of a love that gives itself completely and of a life that is entirely being for others.[52] Non-Christian religions generally see expiation as a matter of restoring the damaged relationship with God by means of conciliatory or expiatory actions offered to God by men. In the New Testament, the situation is reversed: it is not man who goes to God with a compensatory gift, but God who comes to man in order to give to him. God's righteousness is grace: it is he who "restores disturbed right on the initiative of his own power to love, by making unjust man just again, the dead living again, through his own creative mercy".[53] The Cross, then, is, in the first place, a movement from above to below; hence it is to be seen not as a work that man offers to conciliate a wrathful God but as "the expression of that foolish love of God's that gives itself away to the point of humiliation in order thus to save man".[54] Christian worship, accordingly, is, in the first place, thankful acceptance of the divine work of salvation, which occurs primarily in what is fittingly called the Eucharist, "thanksgiving". We do not glorify God by giving something to him out of our own resources, but by letting ourselves be endowed with his own gifts, thus recognizing him as the only Lord.

In addition, the New Testament also points to an ascending interpretation of Christ's sacrifice. The disciples who were initially scandalized by the shameful death of Christ came only slowly to understand its significance by rereading

---

[52] See Ratzinger, *Introduction to Christianity*, 2nd ed. p. 282.
[53] Ibid.
[54] Ibid., p. 283.

the Scriptures in the light of the Christ event. In the various rituals of Israel's religion they found suitable images to explain what had happened. This process is most evident in the Letter to the Hebrews, which connects the death of Jesus on the Cross with the ritual and theology of the Jewish feast of reconciliation and presents it as the true feast of cosmic reconciliation. The sacrifice of bulls and goats is ultimately useless, for God does not seek these but man himself. Only man's unqualified yes to God could form true worship. While everything belongs to God, man has the freedom to say yes or no, to love or to reject. Man's yes, whereby he hands himself back to God, cannot be replaced or represented by the blood of bulls and goats (cf. Heb 8:1–10:18).

However, as all pre-Christian religious cults were based on the notion of substitution or representation and tried to replace the irreplaceable, this worship was bound to remain vain, as the Letter to the Hebrews so devastatingly argues. The same Letter presents Christ as the one true priest. His death, which seemed merely the profane execution of a criminal, is in reality the only true liturgy of the world, which took place not in the material Temple but before the eyes of the world. Through the curtain of death, Christ stepped into the real Temple, the presence of God himself, in order to offer not the blood of animals but himself (cf. Heb 9:11ff.). The Letter to the Hebrews says that Jesus accomplished this expiation through his blood (9:12), by which is meant not a material offering but the concrete expression of a love that extends "to the end" (Jn 13:1). The gesture of a love that gives all: this and this alone was the real means by which the world was reconciled.[55]

[55] See ibid., pp. 286–87.

Christian worship, then, is not a matter of surrendering things to God or destroying them. Rather, as Ratzinger says:

> It consists in the absoluteness of love, as it could only be poured out by the one in whom God's own love had become human love; and it consists in the new form of representation (*Stellvertretung*) included in this love, namely, that he stood for us and that we let ourselves be taken over by him.[56]

In Christian worship, we are called to accept the love of Jesus Christ, who "stands in" for us, to allow ourselves to be united in it and thus become worshippers with him and in him. Christian worship has an "exodus structure", since it involves an abandoning of self in a movement toward God and others through sharing in the worship of Christ, the man "who is all exodus, all self-surpassing love".[57] This implies that Christian worship is the Cross, since it involves being torn apart and dying to self. However, this aspect is secondary to the fundamental characteristic of Christian sacrifice, which is love, and indeed the aspect of destruction only belongs to Christian sacrifice because in a world marked by self-seeking and death, love takes on the form of a force that breaks down, opens up, crucifies, and tears.

As a result, Christ is stretched out on the Cross, from being in God right down to the hell of feeling completely forsaken by God. As Ratzinger puts it, anyone "who has stretched his existence so wide that he is simultaneously immersed in God and in the depths of the God-forsaken creature is bound to be torn asunder, as it were; such a one is truly 'crucified'".[58] This process of being torn apart is

[56] Ibid., p. 287.
[57] Ibid., p. 289.
[58] Ibid., p. 290.

the extreme realization of loving "to the end" (Jn 13:1) and the concrete expression of the breadth love creates.

The Cross, then, should be seen not so much in terms of the intense pain and suffering experienced by Christ but rather as the expression of a love that knows no bounds, of a love that brings God-forsaken man into relation with God. In his love, Jesus reunited the two separated ends of the world (cf. Eph 2:13ff.). The Cross ultimately reveals who God is: he is the God of love prepared to take on human flesh and descend into suffering and death in order to reconcile man to himself. It also reveals to us who man is: he is the sinner who cannot bear the just man and casts him out as a reproach (see Wis 2:12); he is the liar who cannot bear the truth. Yet God descends into this abyss of human failure, revealing the even more inexhaustible abyss of divine love, which judges man by saving him.

Christ's saving work is brought to completion in his Resurrection from the dead. In *Introduction to Christianity*, Joseph Ratzinger takes an anthropological approach to the Resurrection faith, taking the phenomenon of love as his point of departure. Other theologians approach the Resurrection by appeal to human freedom, which tends essentially toward the absolute and finds fulfillment in eternity (e.g., Karl Rahner), to man's tendency to hope beyond death (e.g., Wolfhart Pannenberg), or to his hope for final justice (e.g., Jürgen Moltmann). All of these approaches, including Ratzinger's, conclude that the question of man's purpose in life cannot be answered from within his own history but only eschatologically.[59] Ratzinger begins his reflections on Christ's Resurrection by evoking love's demand for infinity and

---

[59] On these approaches, see Walter Kasper, *Jesus the Christ* (Tunbridge Wells: Burns and Oates; Mahwah, N.J.: Paulist Press, 1976), p. 136.

indestructibility, so well expressed in the Song of Songs: "Love is strong as death" (8:6). But human love cannot satisfy its own cry for infinity, because it is included in the world of death, in its loneliness and its power of destruction. In this context, the message of Christ's Resurrection has particular relevance, for it "is the greater strength of love in the face of death".[60]

Man has no permanence in himself and so, in various ways, he seeks to live on in another, through his offspring or by doing something for which he will be remembered by future generations. Such a form of continued existence is really only a shadow existence, but man's yearning is, in fact, for something greater. Only God can give lasting stability, by taking man up into himself, into his own being. Love is the foundation of immortality and Jesus, the One who loves all, has established immortality for all. For this reason, *his* Resurrection is *our* life. Christ's Resurrection shows that love is stronger than death, and if he has risen, so too have we (cf. 1 Cor 15:16ff.). Our own love, left to itself, is not powerful enough to overcome death; only Christ's love, coinciding with God's own power of life and love, can be the foundation of our immortality.

Christ's new life as the Risen One is qualitatively different from the one he led before his death. He rose to definitive life, which is no longer controlled by the same chemical and biological laws, and is therefore not subject to the possibility of death. There is an element of mystery about his new life, for not all see him, and those who do sometimes fail to recognize him. Only when he opens men's eyes and hearts "can

---

[60] Ratzinger, *Introduction to Christianity*, 2nd ed., p. 302. For an examination of the biblical accounts of the Resurrection of Jesus, see Ratzinger, *Der Gott Jesu Christi*, pp. 150–67, and his *Journey towards Easter*, pp. 110–17.

the countenance of the eternal love that conquers death become recognizable in our mortal world, and, in that love, the
new different world, the world of him who is to come".[61]

Belief in Christ's Resurrection should fill us with joy, for
it teaches us that heaven is not completely sealed off above
the earth. If we grasp the Easter message, then gradually
something of God's light will penetrate our lives, bringing
the joy of Easter in its train:

> Then we shall feel the surge of joy for which otherwise we
> wait in vain. Everyone who is penetrated by something of
> this joy can be, in his own way, a window through which
> heaven can look upon earth and visit it. In this way, what
> Revelation foresees can come about: every creature in heaven
> and on earth and under the earth and in the sea, everything
> in the world, is filled with the joy of the redeemed (cf. Rev
> 5:13). To the extent that we realize this, the words of the
> departing Jesus—who, parting from us, is the coming Jesus—
> are fulfilled: "Your sorrow will turn into joy" (Jn 16:20).
> And like Sarah, people who share an Easter faith can say:
> "God has made me laugh: every one who hears will laugh
> with me" (Gen 21:6).[62]

Faith in the Resurrection of Christ is a confession of the
real existence of God, of his unconditional yes to his creation, of his power over all things, including matter, of his
love, which conquers death and confers new life. The redemptive content of God's revelation on Easter day is that his power
is truly hope and joy. In the midst of a world weighed down
under the threatening shadows of death, this is what gives us
the possibility of joyfully singing the Easter alleluia.[63]

[61] Ratzinger, *Introduction to Christianity*, 2nd ed. p. 308.

[62] Ratzinger, *Behold the Pierced One*, p. 121.

[63] See Ratzinger, *Der Gott Jesu Christi*, p. 167.

Chapter VII

THE SPIRIT OF ETERNAL JOY

While much of Joseph Ratzinger's theological production has been devoted to Jesus Christ, he has written far less about the Holy Spirit.[1] In part, this is probably due to the fact that the third Person of the Blessed Trinity neither makes himself visible nor speaks about himself and is consequently much more mysterious. Given this situation, as Ratzinger says, there is always a risk that theological discussion about the Holy Spirit could be little more than our own abstract speculation, removed from reality.[2]

[1] For Joseph Ratzinger's teaching on the Holy Spirit, see his *Introduction to Christianity*, 2nd ed. (San Francisco: Ignatius Press, 2004), especially pp. 331–37; *Der Gott Jesu Christi: Betrachtungen über den Dreieinigen Gott* (Munich: Kösel, 2006), especially pp. 171–88; "Alcune forme bibliche ed ecclesiali di 'presenza' dello Spirito nella storia", in *Spirito Santo e storia*, ed. L. Sartori (Rome: Ave, 1977), pp. 51–64; "The Holy Spirit as Communion: On the Relationship between Pneumatology and Spirituality in the Writings of Augustine", in *Pilgrim Fellowship of Faith: The Church as Communion* (San Francisco: Ignatius Press, 2005), pp. 38–59 (first published in 1974); "Church Movements and Their Place in Theology", in *Pilgrim Fellowship of Faith*, pp. 176–208 (first published in 1998); "The Holy Spirit and the Church", in *Images of Hope: Meditations on Major Feasts* (San Francisco: Ignatius Press, 2006), pp. 63–73.

[2] On the difficulty of speaking about the Holy Spirit, see Ratzinger, "The Holy Spirit as Communion", p. 38.

The Holy Spirit, however, does not remain distant from us in the mystery of the ineffable Godhead. In fact, the gift of the Spirit is vital for authentic and joyful Christian living. Promised to the apostles at the Last Supper and poured out upon the world following Christ's death and Resurrection, the Holy Spirit satisfies man's ultimate desire for true life and happiness:

> The ultimate thirst of men cries out for the Holy Spirit. He, and he alone, is, at a profound level, the fresh water without which there is no life. In the image of a spring, of the water that irrigates and transforms a desert, that man meets like a secret promise, the mystery of the Spirit becomes visible in an ineffable fashion that no rational meditation can encompass. In man's thirst, and in his being refreshed by water, is portrayed that infinite, far more radical thirst that can be quenched by no other water.[3]

For this reason, there is a secret nostalgia for the Spirit in the heart of man. This nostalgia emerges in Christian prayer, which centers on the basic request for God's gift, which is none other than God himself. In this regard, St. Augustine interprets the petition "Give us this day our daily bread" as a clear reference to the Holy Spirit.[4]

We can come to some understanding of the Holy Spirit by considering him in turn in relation to the Son, the Church, and Christian existence. This division is, as we shall see, not an airtight one, for the mission of Christ is continued in the Church through the power of the Holy Spirit, and a Spirit-filled Christian life is necessarily ecclesial. The Spirit, whom Christ breathed upon the apostles, continually produces love

[3] Ibid., p. 47.

[4] St. Augustine, *De Trinitate*, 5, 14, 15; cf. Ratzinger, "The Holy Spirit as Communion", p. 49.

and joy in human hearts, builds up the communion of the Church, and leads us into the fullness of truth.

1. The Son and the Spirit

The Holy Spirit's mysterious nature makes it easy for man to err in his search for him. As the history of the Church testifies, many erroneous doctrines and radical movements arose on account of the difficulty of knowing the Holy Spirit and failure to pay due attention to the relationship between the Holy Spirit and the other two Persons of the Blessed Trinity. In this context, Joseph Ratzinger makes explicit reference to the heresies of Manicheism and Montanism, and to the spiritual movement sparked by the twelfth-century Calabrian abbot Joachim of Fiore (c. 1130–1202),[5] a figure whom he had studied in some detail while researching for his *Habilitationsschrift* on St. Bonaventure's theology of history. Joachim was acutely aware of the insufficiencies of the Church of his time and came to the conclusion that the Church he knew could not be considered the definitive form of the Church of God on earth. He believed that before Christ's return there would be a fresh intervention of God in history, bringing about a Church in which all would live in spirit and in truth. This belief led to the formulation of his doctrine of three eras in world history, modeled on the Trinitarian understanding of God. Following the reign of the Father in the Old Testament and the reign of the Son in the hierarchical Church, there would

[5] See Ratzinger, *Der Gott Jesu Christi*, pp. 171–78; also his *Gottes Glanz in unserer Zeit: Meditationen zum Kirchenjahr* (Freiburg im Breisgau: Herder, 2005), pp. 108–9, and his *God and the World: A Conversation with Peter Seewald* (San Francisco: Ignatius Press, 2002), p. 362. On the history of Abbot Joachim's influence, see especially Henri de Lubac, *La postérité spirituelle de Joachim de Flore*, 2 vols. (Paris and Namur: Lethielleux, 1979, 1981).

be a new reign of the Holy Spirit, a reign of freedom and universal peace, which, he believed, would come about around the year 1260.

Joachim held that one could take practical steps to bring about the new era, and to this end he set up a new monastic community that he intended as a prefiguration of it. He spoke of the "eternal gospel" (Rev 14:6), the gospel of the Spirit, which is not something other than the gospel of Jesus Christ. Rather, the Holy Spirit would bring it about that the first gospel, the Sermon on the Mount, would finally be applied in its entirety. The gospel taken quite literally would be the new and totally spiritual Christianity.

Abbot Joachim's doctrine was a major inspiration for many early Franciscans, for they saw in it a prophetic prefiguration of St. Francis. However, it led to divisions among them as the original vision was taken over, especially in Italy, by groups who sought to establish a new political order. The abbot's thought continued down through history in ever more corrupted forms. Adolf Hitler's use of the expression "Third Reich" was, in part, mediated through secularized and politicized versions of this thought, as was Marxism's notion that mankind is advancing triumphantly toward the realization of definitive salvation within history itself.

St. Francis of Assisi, however, showed what a true "spiritual" Christianity must be: it consists in living in complete fidelity to the Word of God, without distinctions or compromises. Unlike some of his successors, he was able to distinguish in his own life what truly came from the Spirit from what had other origins. As the example of St. Francis makes clear, the Holy Spirit dwells in the Word, not outside of it; the Word is the place of the Spirit and Jesus is the source of the Spirit. Hence, the more we draw close to Jesus, the more we draw close to the Holy Spirit and the more he enters into us. This link between Jesus and the Holy Spirit shows that there cannot be a utopian kind of Church existing independently of or above the Son.

One cannot know the Spirit by separating him from the Son, but only by immersing oneself in the Son. St. John depicts this in his account of the first appearance of the Risen Jesus to the Eleven: the Spirit is the breath of the Son and we receive him by drawing close to the Son in such a way as to allow him to breathe on us (see Jn 20:19–23). In accordance with the Johannine teaching, St. Irenaeus of Lyons teaches that the Holy Spirit directs and guides in a scarcely perceptible way to the Son and, through him, to the Father.

The Church Fathers teach that the name "Holy Spirit" does not express something specific to the third Person, but what is common in God; all three Persons are spirit and holy. However, as St. Augustine in his treatment of the names of the Holy Spirit argues, it is precisely in this way that what is "proper" to the third Person also emerges.[6] The Spirit is what is common: his particular quality is to be the unity between the Father and the Son, unity in person. The Father and the Son are one thing only in going out of themselves; in the third Person, in the fruitfulness of self-giving, they are one.

Of course, as Ratzinger admits, these affirmations can never be any more than attempts to approach the divine mystery. We can only know the Holy Spirit in the effects he produces, and this is why Scripture never describes the Spirit in himself but speaks only of the way in which he comes to us and how he may be distinguished from other spirits. From the testimony of Scripture, as Ratzinger shows,[7]

[6] See Ratzinger, *Der Gott Jesu Christi*, pp. 179–80; Ratzinger, "The Holy Spirit as Communion", p. 41; St. Augustine, *De Trinitate*, 5, 11, 12–12, 13.
[7] See Ratzinger, *Der Gott Jesu Christi*, pp. 180–88.

we learn that we cannot point to the Holy Spirit as we would to a thing. Referring to John 14:22–31, he explains that only the one who bears the Spirit in himself can see him. The Holy Spirit dwells in the word of Jesus, but one does not obtain this word only by speaking it: one must also observe and live it. The Holy Spirit, who is the life of the Word, thus dwells in the lived word.

In this regard, the early Church, taking its cue from Ephesians 4:8, paid particular attention to Psalm 68 (67), interpreting it as a hymn on the Ascension of Christ and on the sending of the Holy Spirit.[8] The Church Fathers understood Moses' ascent of Sinai as an image of Pentecost. Moses went up not only physically, but also interiorly, exposing himself to solitude with God, which enabled him to bring the Spirit to men in the form of a guiding word. The bringing of the Spirit is the result of his ascent and his solitude. This is but a shadow and prefiguration of what would take place in the New Testament. Jesus really inserted our human nature, human flesh, into communion with God; he brought it through the cloud of death before God's sight. From his Ascension came the Holy Spirit: the outpouring of the Spirit is the result of Christ's victory, the fruit of his love manifested on the Cross.

All of this enables us to say something, even if only haltingly, of the intimate mystery of God. The Father and the Son are a movement of pure self-giving and self-surrender. In this movement, they are fruitful and their fruitfulness is their unity, the fullness of their being one, without detriment or confusion. Ratzinger now invokes the analogy of

---

[8] See ibid., pp. 181–83; also Ratzinger *Gottes Glanz in unserer Zeit*, p. 110. Ratzinger refers in this context to St. Augustine's interpretation of the psalm in *De Trinitate*, 15, 19, 34; see Ratzinger, "The Holy Spirit as Communion", pp. 55–59.

human love, observing that "for us men, self-giving and self-surrender always imply the cross".[9] As he explains elsewhere, there can be no genuine human love without suffering, since love "always demands an element of self-sacrifice, because, given temperamental differences and the drama of situations, it will always bring with it renunciation and pain".[10] Applying this to God, who is love, Ratzinger concludes that "the Trinitarian mystery manifests itself in this world in the mystery of the Cross: in it is the fruitfulness from which the Holy Spirit comes." [11]

St. John makes it clear that the Holy Spirit does not dwell separately from the Word but in it. He describes the Spirit's activity in history as one of "reminding". The Spirit does not speak from what is his but from what is Christ's.[12] He is recognized in his fidelity to the Word, which has already been spoken. John's theology of the Holy Spirit is constructed in parallel with his Christology, for Christ's teaching is also characterized by the fact that it is not his own but is of the One who sent him (see Jn 7:16). This form of existence, which is completely devoid of self-interest and is for the other, legitimizes him before the world. In contrast, the Antichrist may be recognized from the fact that he speaks only in his own name. The Spirit shows himself to be the Trinitarian Spirit because he does not appear as a separate and separable "I", but "disappears" into the Father and the Son. Against the Gnostic claim to secret knowledge, John emphasizes in his teaching on the Holy Spirit that there cannot be a new revelation that differs from that already given by the Word.

---

[9] Ratzinger, *Der Gott Jesu Christi*, p. 183.
[10] Ratzinger, *God and the World*, p. 322.
[11] Ratzinger, *Der Gott Jesu Christi*, p. 183.
[12] See ibid.; also Ratzinger, "The Holy Spirit as Communion", p. 39.

In this context, John draws attention to the ecclesial nature of faith. In the Church, one does not speak one's own word but "disappears" into the ecclesial "we". The entire fourth Gospel is intended to be nothing other than an act of "reminding" and, for this reason, it is a pneumatic or spiritual Gospel. It is fruitful, new and profound, precisely because it does not seek new systems but limits itself to reminding. The essence of the Holy Spirit, as the unity between the Father and the Son, lies in the altruism of reminding, which is true renewal. The pneumatic Church is not something other than the Church founded by Christ but one that, in remembering, understands more deeply, immerses herself more profoundly in the Word, and becomes richer and more dynamic.

Ratzinger finds confirmation of St. John's teaching in the Letters of St. Paul.[13] In the community at Corinth, St. Paul found himself facing a situation of almost infantile joy for the gifts of the Spirit, which was, however, beginning to pose a threat to their authenticity. To overcome the spirit of rivalry and superficiality that was becoming evident in the community, Paul reminded the Corinthians that only one gift is necessary, namely, love (see 1 Cor 13). Without it, everything else is vain. Love, however, is expressed in unity, which is opposed to any form of sect mentality. It is manifested in building up the community and bearing with one another. The one who builds is the Holy Spirit. Where there is bitterness, jealousy, hostility, the Spirit is not present. A knowledge deprived of love does not come from him. This Pauline teaching is similar to St. John's doctrine that love is manifested in the abiding of the Spirit.

[13] See Ratzinger, *Der Gott Jesu Christi*, pp. 186–88.

Elsewhere, Ratzinger, drawing on St. Augustine's teaching in the *De Trinitate*, explains that the fundamental activity of the Holy Spirit, who is love, is to unite and draw into abiding unity:

> Love shows itself by being enduring. It can by no means be recognized at a given moment and in the moment alone; but in abiding, it does away with uncertainty and carries eternity within it. And thus ... the relationship between love and truth is also thereby given: love, in the full sense, can be present only where something is enduring, where something abides. Because it has to do with abiding, it can occur, not just anywhere, but only there where eternity is.[14]

This indicates that the Spirit is not to be sought in discontinuity, in what is always unpredictable. Rather, he dwells in what is "abiding", in enduring and creative faithfulness. The Spirit shows his credentials, so to speak, in bringing to remembrance (see Jn 14:26) and in unifying.

There is another point of contact between Paul and John. John describes the Spirit as the Paraclete, which means he is the advocate, helper, defender, and consoler. He is God's yes to man, just as Christ is. Corresponding to this teaching is the strong emphasis that Paul places on joy. As Ratzinger puts it, the Holy Spirit is the Spirit of joy, of the gospel (cf. Gal 5:22). Joy is a sign of the Holy Spirit's presence and thus of grace: where joy and humor are lacking, the Spirit cannot be present. A person who is profoundly serene, who has suffered without losing joy, cannot be far from the God of the gospel, from the Spirit of God, who is the Spirit of eternal joy.[15]

[14] Ratzinger, "The Holy Spirit as Communion", p. 45; cf. ibid., pp. 54–55.
[15] See Ratzinger, *Der Gott Jesu Christi*, p. 188.

2. The Spirit and the Church

As the *Catechism of the Catholic Church* explains, the Spirit who "has spoken through the prophets" makes us hear the Father's Word, but he does not speak of himself.[16] We come to know him as he reveals the Word to us and disposes us to welcome him in faith. At the Last Supper, Jesus promised the gift of the Holy Spirit, who would lead the apostles and their successors into the fullness of truth.

The Church is the place where we are able to know the Holy Spirit: "in the Scriptures he inspired; in the Tradition"; in the "Magisterium, which he assists; in the sacramental liturgy", in which he places us in "communion with Christ; in prayer, wherein he intercedes for us; in the charisms and ministries by which the Church is built up; in the signs of apostolic and missionary life; [and] in the witness of the saints through whom he manifests his holiness and continues the work of salvation." [17]

In his commentary on the Apostles' Creed, Joseph Ratzinger points out that its third section refers to the Holy Spirit not in the first place as the third Person of the Trinity but as God's gift to history in the community of those who believe in Christ.[18] Of course, the reference to the Triune God is not excluded: after all, the creeds grew out of the threefold baptismal question about faith in the Father, Son, and Holy Spirit, a question that for its part rests on the baptismal formula recorded in St. Matthew's Gospel (see 28:19).

The Creed thus speaks not of God's inner life, but of "God facing outwards", of the Holy Spirit as "the power through which the risen Lord remains present in the history of the

---

[16] See *Catechism of the Catholic Church*, no. 687.

[17] Ibid., no. 688.

[18] See Ratzinger, *Introduction to Christianity*, 2nd ed., p. 331.

world as the principle of a new history and a new world".[19]
Elsewhere, noting a tendency in some circles to separate Christology from pneumatology, Ratzinger stresses that one cannot understand the Holy Spirit in separation from Christ.
Although Christ and the Holy Spirit are not the same person, it is true to say that Christ's continued presence among
us is due to the fact that "he has gone before us in the way
of life of the Holy Spirit and shares himself through him and
in him."[20] In this way, Ratzinger draws attention to the
link between Christ, the Holy Spirit, and the Church. The
Church is to be understood by reference not only to Christ
but also to the Holy Spirit. This double reference has important consequences for a renewed ecclesiology:

> Teaching about the Church must take its departure from
> teaching about the Holy Spirit and his gifts. But its goal
> lies in a doctrine of the history of God with men or, alter-
> natively, of the function of the story of Christ for mankind
> as a whole. This indicates at the same time in what direc-
> tion Christology must evolve. It is not to be developed as a
> doctrine of God's taking root in the world, a doctrine that,
> starting from Jesus' humanity, interprets the Church in an
> all too worldly fashion. Christ remains present through the
> Holy Spirit with all his openness and breadth and freedom,
> which by no means exclude the institutional form but limit
> its claims and do not allow it simply to make itself the same
> as worldly institutions.[21]

In the third section of the Creed, the remaining statements
are intended to be nothing more than developments of the

[19] Ibid., pp. 332–33.

[20] Ratzinger, "Church Movements and Their Place in Theology",
pp. 183–84.

[21] Ratzinger, *Introduction to Christianity*, 2nd ed., pp. 333–34.

basic profession of belief in the Holy Spirit. Belief in the communion of saints and in the forgiveness of sins is connected with belief in the Holy Spirit's way of working in history.

The communion of saints (*communio sanctorum*) is, in the first place, the Eucharistic community, which through the body of the Lord binds the churches scattered throughout the world into one Church. The word *sanctorum* originally referred not to persons (*sancti*) but to the holy things (*sancta*) granted to the Church in her Eucharistic feast as the real bond of unity. The Church is thus defined not as a matter of offices or organization but in sacramental terms on the basis of her Eucharistic worship. This led to the inclusion of the persons who are united with God and one another through the Eucharist. In this way, the Church came to be seen not only as the unity of the Eucharistic table but also as the community of those who are united through the Eucharist. This quickly acquired a cosmic breadth: the communion of saints extends beyond the confines of death to embrace all who have received the one Spirit and his life-giving power.

The phrase about the forgiveness of sins refers to the other fundamental sacrament of the Church, namely, baptism, and it very soon came to refer also to the sacrament of penance. One becomes a Christian not by birth but rebirth: man must abandon the self-satisfaction of mere existence and turn his life around. In this sense, baptism, as the start of a life-long process of conversion, establishes the fundamental pattern of Christian life. All of this is made possible through the inner working of the Holy Spirit.

In his article "The Holy Spirit as Communion", Ratzinger refers to the pneumatological Christology of St. Paul and the farewell discourses of the fourth Gospel to conclude that the new presence of Christ in the Spirit is the necessary presupposition for the sacraments and the Lord's presence in them. In this sense, we could say that the Holy Spirit links Christ and the Church, for it is he who ensures the continued efficacy of Christ's saving presence in the Church and her sacraments. The Spirit dwells in the Church, sanctifying her continuously through the sacraments, guiding her to a deeper understanding of the Word entrusted to her, and ensuring that love continues to inspire the Church's activity.[22]

The Church is thus the center of the Holy Spirit's activity in the world. The Apostles' Creed approaches the mystery of the Church from the two angles of baptism/penance and the Eucharist. This leads to a God-centered conception of the Church, based on the operation of the Holy Spirit, who brings about the conversion and unification of those who belong to the Church. Forgiveness leads to communion, and Eucharistic communion leads to the communion of the converted "who all eat one and the same bread, to become in it 'one body' (1 Cor 10:17) and, indeed, 'one single new man' (cf. Eph 2:15)".[23]

Similarly, Ratzinger emphasizes that not only the various charisms and spiritual movements that arise from time to time in the Church, but also her spiritual office, which the tradition has framed in the concept of "apostolic succession", are essentially linked to the working of the Holy Spirit at all times in the Church.[24] Consequently, although tensions may arise, there can be no ultimate irreconcilable conflict between them. Apostolic succession does not mean that we have become somehow independent of the Holy Spirit on account of the unbroken line of succession. Rather, the succession is dependent on the sacrament of holy orders,

[22] See Ratzinger, "The Holy Spirit as Communion", p. 54.

[23] Ratzinger, *Introduction to Christianity*, 2nd ed., p. 336.

[24] See Ratzinger, "Church Movements and Their Place in Theology", p. 184.

which means that it is not something we can provide for ourselves but must be given again and again by the Spirit. The Lord, through the gift of the Spirit, has reserved to himself the institution and constant renewal of the priestly ministry. In this, we see the connection between the "once" of the origins of the priestly ministry in Christ's work and the "always" of the sacrament, the presence in all the ages of the Church of the historical origins, which is the work of the Spirit. The Holy Spirit's work is always intimately bound up with the work of Christ, with God's actions in history. At the same time, the Holy Spirit makes it possible for the once-for-all element (cf. Heb 7:27) to be present and endure for ever. By the power of the Spirit, who works in so many different ways in the life of the Church, Christ can be present in all times and all places.

The concluding words of the Creed profess belief in "the resurrection of the body" and "life everlasting"; these words "are to be understood as the unfolding of faith in the Holy Spirit and his transforming power, whose final effect they depict".[25] The prospect of resurrection follows from faith in the transformation of history that began with the Resurrection of Christ. The conviction that the barrier of death has been broken through is one in which faith in Christ and acknowledgment of the power of the Holy Spirit meet and is expressly applied in the last words of the Creed to the future of us all.

3. The Holy Spirit and Christian existence

In his article "The Holy Spirit and the Church", originally published in 1989, Joseph Ratzinger shows how the Holy

---

[25] Ratzinger, *Introduction to Christianity*, 2nd ed., p. 336.

Spirit builds up a new humanity within the Church in the image of the Trinity, and he describes what authentic Christian living must be. The Holy Spirit is neither an isolated entity nor one that can be isolated; rather, his nature is to refer us to the unity of the Triune God.[26] His task in the history of salvation and, therefore, in the Church is to lead us to this unity. The Triune God is the model or archetype (*Urbild*) of a new, united humanity, and the archetype of the Church, for whose unity, modeled on that of the Trinity, Christ prayed (cf. Jn 17:11). In the Church, mankind, which had become the antithetical image of God through its disunity, can return to being the one Adam. Since the Trinity is the archetype of renewed mankind and of the Church, the Church is not an extra idea added to man, but provides the context in which man can become fully man. Because the Holy Spirit manifests the unity of God, he must be the vital element of the Church, in which opposites are mutually reconciled and the scattered fragments of Adam return to unity.

As Ratzinger argues, we can bring about unity among ourselves only if we find ourselves in a deeper unity, in a third, as it were: only if we are one with God can we be united with one another. Otherwise, we remain eternally separated from one another by a gulf that no amount of goodwill can bridge. Experience teaches that this is no abstract theory. Rarely as in our time have people become so dramatically aware of how inaccessible others ultimately are and of how difficult it is to give oneself to another or understand the other in an enduring way.

Pentecost, says Ratzinger, is the response to this situation. The Spirit sheds light on the fundamental human question "How can we reach one another?" More specifically,

[26] See Ratzinger, "The Holy Spirit and the Church", p. 63.

how is it possible to remain oneself and yet leave the prison of one's solitude to encounter the other from within? The answer lies neither in a dissolution of self, after the manner of some of the Asiatic religions, nor in simple activism. Furthermore, the "I" and the "you" cannot be reconciled with each other if the "I" is not reconciled with itself.

The Christian answer is to be found in the Trinity, which is the highest unity. In the Trinity, the oppositeness of the "I" and the "you" is not taken away; instead, a mutual compenetration takes place in the Holy Spirit.[27] God did not create man for ultimate dissolution but so that he might open himself out in all his height and depth, where the Holy Spirit embraces him and is the unity that overcomes the separateness of individuals.[28]

The Church in her essence, because of the activity of the Holy Spirit, is the overcoming of the boundaries between "I" and "you"; she is the place where man comes to share in the kind of life that characterizes the Triune God. Her mission is therefore to all mankind: she must bring into unity the scattered children of God (cf. Jn 11:52).[29] This process, as Ratzinger points out elsewhere, begins with Christ's being raised on the Cross, which leads to the outpouring of the Holy Spirit of unity on his disciples.[30]

Being Christian entails breaking out of one's isolated self (*Aufbrechen*) and allowing oneself to be broken open (*Aufgebrochenwerden*) so that one's capacity can be released like the grain of wheat that dies and, in being opened out, bears fruit (cf. Jn 12:24). To become a Christian means to be

[27] On this theme, see Ratzinger, *Introduction to Christianity*, 2nd ed., pp. 184–90.

[28] See Ratzinger, "The Holy Spirit and the Church", p. 68.

[29] See ibid., p. 69.

[30] See Ratzinger, *Introduction to Christianity*, 2nd ed., pp. 239–40.

brought into unity (*Christwerden ist ein Vereinigtwerden*): the fragments of the shattered image of Adam must be joined together. Thus, to be a Christian is not a form of self-affirmation but involves setting out on the path that leads to the unity that embraces all of mankind in every time and place.

While the Holy Spirit is the spirit of unity, it is also true that he is given to each one personally and in a particular way; this truth is symbolized by the flames of fire at the first Pentecost, which separated and came to rest on the heads of each one (see Acts 2:3).[31] Christ assumed human nature, which unites us all, and it is from that nature that he brings us together into unity. The Spirit, however, is given to each one of us personally: through him, Christ becomes the personal response for each one of us in turn. The unity among individuals in the Church does not take place through the dissolving of the person but by bringing him to fulfillment, which means that he is opened up in an unlimited way.

At this point, Ratzinger draws the consequences for authentic ecclesial existence, which builds on his notion of the person as essentially related to God and to others. On the one hand, no one acts in the Church simply of his own volition: each one must act, speak, and think according to the communion of the new "we" of the Church, which exists in a relationship of exchange with the "we" of the Triune God. On the other hand, no one acts simply as the representative of a group or collective system: each one exercises personal responsibility in accordance with his conscience, which has been opened up and purified in the faith. Such a conscience, says Ratzinger, does not invent but derives its creativity from what is received in common in the faith.

[31] See also Ratzinger, *God and the World*, p. 349.

To speak or act as a Christian means that one is never simply an isolated self. To become a Christian entails accepting the Church in her entirety into oneself or, more precisely, it means allowing oneself to be interiorly accepted into her. In this situation, the Spirit is able to express himself and bring about a broadening of the individual's views and an interior openness to the other; all of this is required for genuine encounter with the other.

To be a Christian implies conversion, which is not simply a question of changing one's ideas but involves a dying to oneself.[32] The "I" loses itself in order to find itself in a greater subject that embraces heaven and earth, past, present, and future, and, for this reason, is in contact with truth itself. The Holy Spirit, who is fire, brings about man's conversion: he overcomes the mortal solitude of the "I" closed in on itself and brings about the opening of self and its fusion with the new subject that is the body of Christ or the Church. Each one receives the Holy Spirit in a particular way, and so each one is a Christian in a unique and unrepeatable fashion. At the same time, because the Spirit is one, we can turn through him to one another to form together the one Church.

Faith itself is a flame of fire that burns, transforms, and recasts us, and so the "I" exists in the paradoxical situation of being "I", yet not "I". That said, whoever meets the average Christian today is bound to ask "Where has the flame gone?" The run-of-the-mill Christian seems rather lukewarm. Rather than allowing ourselves to be burnt by the fire of faith, the fire of the Holy Spirit, we tend to

[32] On this theme, see also Joseph Ratzinger, "Faith as Conversion—Metanoia", in *Principles of Catholic Theology* (San Francisco: Ignatius Press, 1987), pp. 55–67.

reduce faith to a vision of the world made to our own measure, with the intention of inflicting no damage on our own comfort and sparing ourselves the trouble of protesting about matters that scarcely upset our daily habits.

However, whenever we dodge the burning fire of the Holy Spirit, Christian existence is only apparently comfortable. As Joseph Ratzinger puts it, "The comfort of the individual is the discomfort of the whole."[33] Where there is unwillingness to expose oneself to the fire of God, frictions become more and more unbearable, and the Church, to use St. Basil's expression, ends up torn apart by the shouting and strife of rival parties.[34]

In *God and the World* Ratzinger speaks of how the Holy Spirit responds to situations where Christians lack energy and zeal. Admitting that even Church leaders can always be tempted to accommodate themselves to the spirit of the age, he goes on to point out that, where this happens, the Holy Spirit "always puts us to shame by bringing the needed renewal from quite a different direction".[35] In this context, he cites the examples of the great saints of the Catholic Counter-Reformation: Teresa of Avila, John of the Cross, Ignatius of Loyola, and Philip Neri. While the Church can become tired and even disappear in certain regions, we have the assurance that, because the Lord Jesus will always be with her, acting through the power of the Spirit, the Church will continue to be, until the end of time, "his special sphere of action, his organism, his Body and his vine".[36]

Only if we do not fear the flame of fire and the tempest it brings with it will the Church truly become the

[33] Ratzinger, "The Holy Spirit and the Church", p. 73.
[34] See St. Basil, *On the Holy Spirit*, 30, 77 (PG 32: 213A).
[35] Ratzinger, *God and the World*, p. 361.
[36] Ibid.

icon of the Holy Spirit. Only then, Ratzinger says, will she open the world to the light of God. The Church began when the disciples were united in prayer in the Upper Room, awaiting the descent of the Holy Spirit. This is how the Church is constantly renewed, and it is for this gift that we should constantly pray when we invoke the Holy Spirit.[37]

[37] See Ratzinger, "The Holy Spirit and the Church", p. 73.

Chapter VIII

THE CHURCH, GUARDIAN OF JOY

Joy is dependent on truth, and the Church is "the living agent carrying the truth of Christ".[1] Since she is in the service of truth and love, the Church is also the servant, guardian, and teacher of joy. She exists in order that the world may come to know true joy, which is found only in God. As Joseph Ratzinger says, the Church's great gift to mankind, her service to joy, lies in the "comfort of the Word and of the sacraments that she provides in good and bad days alike".[2]

The Church can be adequately understood only when she is seen not in sociological terms as a merely human construction that can be modified and transformed at will in accordance with the needs and fashions of the age, but as a supernatural mystery, a gift to mankind, which has been brought into being according to the eternal plan of the Trinitarian God.[3] Her mission is essentially that of continuing

[1] Joseph Ratzinger, *God and the World: A Conversation with Peter Seewald* (San Francisco: Ignatius Press, 2002), p. 355.

[2] Joseph Ratzinger, *Introduction to Christianity*, 2nd ed. (San Francisco: Ignatius Press, 2004), p. 343.

[3] See Ratzinger, *God and the World*, pp. 342–43; Second Vatican Council, Dogmatic Constitution on the Church, *Lumen Gentium*, November 21, 1964, nos. 2–4.

Christ's work of salvation and redemption in our regard. The Church is at the service of our authentic freedom. By opening a window onto God and the eternal, she takes us beyond the limitations of this world, points to the depths of the great mystery that is man, and indicates the way that leads to true life and fulfillment.

The Church necessarily has a visible organization, some aspects of which, being manmade, are open to change depending on historical needs and circumstances. However, since her fundamental sacramental and hierarchical structures are willed by God, and since her basic teaching is not her own but God's, these are inviolable.[4] In this regard, all the Church's members are bound to the word and the will of the One who is our Lord and our freedom.[5] Having said that, the Church's concrete structures are not the main focus of attention for those who truly believe and receive from her the gift of faith, which for them is life:

> Only someone who has experienced how, regardless of changes in her ministers and forms, the Church raises men up, gives them a home and a hope, a home that is hope—the path to eternal life—only someone who has experienced this knows what the Church is, both in days gone by and now.[6]

Beginning with his doctoral thesis on the ecclesiology of St. Augustine, Joseph Ratzinger has made many significant contributions to the theology of the Church.[7] While he

[4] See Joseph Ratzinger and Vittorio Messori, *The Ratzinger Report: An Exclusive Interview on the State of the Church* (San Francisco: Ignatius Press, 1985), p. 46.

[5] See Joseph Ratzinger, *Called to Communion: Understanding the Church Today* (San Francisco: Ignatius Press, 1996), p. 146.

[6] Ratzinger, *Introduction to Christianity*, 2nd ed., p. 344.

[7] For example, see the following works by Joseph Ratzinger: *Das Neue Volk Gottes: Entwürfe zur Ekklesiologie* (Düsseldorf: Patmos, 1969), which has

has written much on the Church's institutions, structures, and ministries and has on occasion made proposals for reform and improvement, he stresses that all of these are, ultimately, in the category of means, rather than ends; they are directed to the Church's God-given mission of salvation in the world, a mission of truth and love that is a true service to joy. True or real reform, he says,

> is to strive to let what is ours disappear as much as possible so what belongs to Christ may become more visible. It is a truth well known to the saints. Saints, in fact, reformed the Church in depth, not by working up plans for new structures but by reforming themselves. What the Church needs in order to respond to the needs of man in every age is holiness, not management.[8]

In his 1990 lecture "A Company in Constant Renewal",[9] delivered at the annual meeting organized in Rimini, Italy, by the *Comunione e Liberazione* movement, Joseph Ratzinger described true reform as a removal of what hinders us from perceiving the noble form of the Church, in order that the light of God himself may shine through. When this happens, God is able to draw us, through the Church's ministry, out of our own isolation into the communion of the body of Christ. Church renewal has both personal and communitarian dimensions. At all levels, it calls in the first

---

not yet been translated into English; *Church, Ecumenism and Politics: New Essays in Ecclesiology* (Slough: St. Paul Publications, 1988); *Called to Communion*; and *Pilgrim Fellowship of Faith: The Church as Communion* (San Francisco: Ignatius Press, 2005). For a discussion of Ratzinger's theology of the Church, see Maximilian Heinrich Heim, *Joseph Ratzinger: Life in the Church and Living Theology. Fundamentals of Ecclesiology with reference to* Lumen Gentium (San Francisco: Ignatius Press, 2007).

[8] Ratzinger, *The Ratzinger Report*, p. 53.

[9] This lecture is contained in Ratzinger, *Called to Communion*, pp. 133–56.

place for the act of faith, which breaks through the barriers of finitude imposed by the positivist and pragmatist thinking of our age and thus creates the open space that reaches into the unlimited and eternal reality that is God.[10] Without faith, any reform would be a mere tinkering with manmade structures to achieve purely human aims; with it, we possess the criterion enabling us to engage in genuine renewal as God wills it.

At the personal level, we need to remove the incrustation that prevents the noble form of the image of God, according to which we are made, from being seen. We need God's forgiveness, which Christ constantly makes available to us, and we must set out on the path of conversion, which requires moral renewal and expiation for our sins, as Christ teaches us. Forgiveness, penance, and following Christ as a disciple lie at the heart of personal renewal and make it possible for us to give witness to God in a way that is attractive and convincing.

God's grace and personal conversion are also essential to the renewal of the community of the Church. Through them the individual becomes one with Christ (cf. Gal 2:20) and is incorporated into the communion of his body, the Church, which embraces all those who in every time and place believed in Christ, hoped in him, and loved him. By placing our faith in God and committing ourselves to personal renewal, we also contribute to the ongoing renewal of the Church, which continues unceasingly though the ages under the guidance of the Holy Spirit, who constantly makes all things new.[11]

---

[10] See ibid., p. 144.

[11] This paragraph summarizes, all too briefly, what Ratzinger says in ibid., pp. 147–56.

Joseph Ratzinger's theology of the Church may be described as a Eucharistic ecclesiology, or an ecclesiology of communion. Influenced by St. Paul and the Fathers of the Church, especially St. Augustine, he sees the Church essentially as a communion, a unity that is more profound than any form of external collectivism since it "reaches deep into the heart of man and endures even in death".[12] In this world, only the Church "goes beyond even the radically impassable frontier: the frontier of death. Living or dead, the members of the Church live in association with the same life that proceeds from the incorporation of all in the Body of Christ."[13]

Through baptism, a person is incorporated into the one body of Christ; he receives the sacrament from "the community of those who have believed before him and who tell him of God as an accepted reality of their history".[14] Baptism is not a purely individual affair but has an essential ecclesial dimension: to be born of God "means to be born of the whole Christ, Head and members".[15] The company of believers, entered through baptism, is continuously built up through faithful listening to God's Word and through the celebration of the sacraments, especially the Eucharist. The Church, in the final analysis, says Ratzinger, *is* Eucharist:

> The Church is *communio*; she is God's communing with men in Christ and hence the communing of men with one another—and, in consequence, sacrament, sign, instrument of salvation. The Church is the celebration of the Eucharist; the Eucharist is the Church; they do not simply stand side

[12] Joseph Ratzinger, "The Church as the Sacrament of Salvation", in *Principles of Catholic Theology* (San Francisco: Ignatius Press, 1987), p. 53.

[13] Ratzinger, *The Ratzinger Report*, p. 48.

[14] Ratzinger, "Baptism, Faith and Membership in the Church—the Unity of Structure and Content", in *Principles of Catholic Theology*, p. 30.

[15] Ibid., p. 33.

by side; they are one and the same. The Eucharist is the
sacramentum Christi, and, because the Church is *Eucharistia*,
she is therefore also *sacramentum*—the sacrament to which
all the other sacraments are ordered.[16]

According to Ratzinger, all the essential elements of the
Christian notion of communion are to be found in 1 John
1:3–4: "That which we have seen and heard we proclaim
also to you, so that you may have fellowship [*koinōnia*] with
us; and our fellowship is with the Father and with his Son
Jesus Christ. And we are writing this that our joy may be
complete." [17] Encounter with the incarnate Son of God is
the starting point of fellowship or communion. Christ comes
to us through the preaching of the Church, which gives rise
to the fellowship of the faithful with one another. This fellowship, in turn, is dependent upon fellowship with the Trinitarian God:

> Fellowship with God is mediated by the fellowship of God
> with man, which is Christ in person; the encounter with
> Christ brings about fellowship with him and, thus, with
> the Father in the Holy Spirit; on this basis it unites men
> with one another. All this is directed toward perfect joy:
> the Church bears within herself an eschatological impulse.[18]

Mention of perfect joy in 1 John 1:4 links this verse with
the farewell discourses of Jesus, and thus with the Paschal
mystery in its entirety and with the Lord's return after his
Resurrection and at the end of time (cf. Jn 16:20–24). Com-
paring John 16:24 ("Until now you have asked nothing in
my name; ask, and you will receive, that your joy may be

[16] Ratzinger, "The Church as the Sacrament of Salvation", p. 53.
[17] See Ratzinger, "The Ecclesiology of the Constitution *Lumen Gentium*",
in *Pilgrim Fellowship of Faith*, p. 130.
[18] Ibid.

full") and Luke 11:13 ("If you then, who are evil, know how to give good gifts to your children, how much more will the heavenly Father give the Holy Spirit to those who ask him!"), Ratzinger argues that "joy" and the "Holy Spirit" ultimately mean the same thing and that the Holy Spirit, who is otherwise not explicitly mentioned, is indicated by the saying about joy in 1 John 1:4.

The notion of communion, then, has a deep theological, Christological, and ecclesiological meaning, connected as it is with the Trinity, Christ, the history of salvation, and the Church. As a result, it also has a sacramental meaning, which emerges clearly in St. Paul: "The cup of blessing which we bless, is it not a participation [koinōnia] in the blood of Christ? The bread which we break, is it not a participation in the body of Christ? Because there is one bread, we who are many are one body, for we all partake of the one bread" (1 Cor 10:16–17). In the Eucharist, Christ continually gives himself to us, and in this way he builds up the Church as his body and unites us with God and with one another.[19]

From all of this it is clear that the Church is, as it were (veluti), the sacrament, that is, the sign and instrument of union with God,[20] and hence of the mutual union of the faithful in a single movement of love for him. The Church's mission is essentially religious rather than political. That said, while her task is not directly that of establishing world peace or unity among peoples, her unity is a constant incentive for the realization of these ideals.[21] In other words, although

[19] See ibid., pp. 130–32.

[20] See Second Vatican Council, Dogmatic Constitution on the Church, Lumen Gentium, no. 1.

[21] See Ratzinger, "The Church as the Sacrament of Salvation", pp. 53–54; Gérard Philips, L'Église et son mystère au IIe Concile du Vatican (Paris: Desclée, 1967), p. 74.

one must distinguish between working for a unified temporal order in the earthly realm and building up the universal kingdom of Christ, one cannot deny the interaction
between the two. In accordance with the principle "Render ... to Caesar the things that are Caesar's, and to God
the things that are God's" (Mt 22:21), the Church does not
seek to establish a theocracy that would dictate how the
social, economic, or political domain should be organized.
At the same time, there is no doubt that faith can have a
profound and beneficial effect on the progress of the temporal realm and that the Church has a duty to make her
own specific contribution to the promotion of the common good.[22]

With regard to the Church's primary religious mission,
one of Joseph Ratzinger's more recent and significant contributions is his article "The Church on the Threshold of
the Third Millennium".[23] In it, he begins by contrasting
the joy of Christian faith with the bleakness of hell. Hell,
he says, is the situation where God is absent. Beyond any
hell that could have been imagined in the past, as for example in Dante Alighieri's *Inferno*, the hells of the twentieth
century sought to bring about a future world where man
would be his own master, no longer needing God.

In contrast, the fundamental Christian task is to witness
to God, for where God is acknowledged, life is bright and
meaningful. Christian faith means being touched by God

[22] On these themes, see the various essays collected in Ratzinger, *Church,
Ecumenism and Politics*; Joseph Ratzinger, *Christianity and the Crisis of Cultures*
(San Francisco: Ignatius Press, 2006); Joseph Ratzinger, *Values in a Time of
Upheaval* (New York: Crossroad; San Francisco: Ignatius Press, 2006). See also
Joseph Ratzinger and Marcello Pera, *Without Roots: The West, Relativism, Chris-
tianity and Islam* (New York: Basic Books, 2006).

[23] This article is contained in Ratzinger, *Pilgrim Fellowship of Faith*,
pp. 284–98.

and witnessing to him. The Church exists so that man can know God and live in fellowship with him in a relationship where God freely gives his love and receives a response of love; she exists in order to prevent the advance of hell on earth and to make the earth a fit place to live in through the light of God. The Church is not there for her own sake, but for mankind: she is there "so that the world may become a sphere for God's presence, the sphere of the covenant between God and men".[24]

The Church serves the world by the fact that God dwells within her; she enables him to be seen and she carries him to mankind. She carries out this mission in various ways. Ratzinger singles out certain tasks as particularly urgent.

First, the Church needs to revive the argument of the rationality of faith, in line with Pope John Paul II's teaching in the encyclical *Fides et Ratio*.[25] Everyone has a deep-rooted capacity to know God; this can be awakened by faith's appeal to reason, to the transparency of creation in revealing the Creator. Where faith and reason part company, both become diseased: atrophied or amputated reason becomes cold and cruel, since it no longer recognizes anything superior to it, and faith, reduced to a matter of feeling, descends into a sick form of religiosity, which ultimately fails to satisfy man's deep-seated desire to know the truth.[26]

Of course, as Ratzinger says, the revelation in creation to which St. Paul refers (see Acts 17:16–34; Rom 1:20) does not suffice to bring man into relationship with God.[27] By

[24] Ibid., p. 287.

[25] On this point, see Joseph Ratzinger, *Truth and Tolerance: Christian Belief and World Religions* (San Francisco: Ignatius Press, 2004), pp. 183–209.

[26] See ibid., pp. 156–61.

[27] See Ratzinger, *Pilgrim Fellowship of Faith*, p. 292.

this, he seems to mean that outside of revealed religion, man cannot enjoy the unique kind of relationship with God that is made possible by God's grace and is characterized by knowledge and love of God as he truly is.[28] However, Ratzinger does not intend to exclude other kinds of relationship with God that fall short of this.

Man is continually in search of God. He can come to know something of God through reason and through the traces of God found in creation and in the world's religions, though such knowledge is always prone to error. Although man can relate to God in an imperfect way outside of revealed religion through different forms of prayer and worship, these human strivings do not enable him to encounter God as Father. This does not preclude his being saved, in a manner known to God alone.[29] However, "if the God who has been discovered by thinking appears within a religion, as a God who speaks and who acts, then thought and faith have been reconciled." [30] Christianity teaches that in his only begotten Son, Jesus Christ, God has in fact come to meet man, that he "has shown him his face, opened up his heart to him".[31] Indeed, God invites man to enjoy a privileged relationship with him as an adopted son; this is brought about through baptism. The Church, then, must make God more widely known; she exists in order to bring God to man and man to God.

---

[28] Divine revelation makes it possible for Christians to possess true and error-free knowledge of God in this life, though it falls short of the knowledge of God possessed by the saints in heaven, who see the very essence of God. On this subject, see St. Thomas Aquinas, *Summa Theologiae*, I, q. 12.

[29] See *Catechism of the Catholic Church*, nos. 836–48.

[30] Ratzinger, *Truth and Tolerance*, p. 171; cf. Joseph Ratzinger, *Behold the Pierced One: An Approach to a Spiritual Christology* (San Francisco: Ignatius Press, 1986), pp. 27–32.

[31] Ratzinger, *Pilgrim Fellowship of Faith*, p. 292.

According to Ratzinger, the great and central task of the Church today, as it ever was, is to show people the path to Christ and to God, and to offer a pilgrim fellowship in walking it.[32] Knowledge of God is a path that requires not only the understanding, but also the will and the heart, in short, our whole being. Religion cannot be pigeonholed into a particular area, for it exists "to integrate man in his entirety, to unite feeling, understanding and will and to mediate between them, and to offer some answer to the demand made by everything as a whole, the demands of living and dying, of society and myself, of present and future".[33]

Ratzinger sees in the Lucan account of the disciples journeying to Emmaus (see Lk 24:13–35) a portrayal of the Christian path toward God, which is a "traveling together with Christ the living Word, who interprets for us the written word, the Bible, and turns that into the path, the path along which our heart starts to burn and ... our eyes are finally opened".[34] Three things belong together on this path, just as they belong to the Church in all ages: the fellowship of the disciples, the Scriptures, and the living presence of Christ made manifest in the breaking of bread. It must become possible for all to experience the Church as a pilgrim fellowship "with our cares, with the word of God, and with Christ" and this fellowship "has to lead us onward

[32] In this regard, Ratzinger refers elsewhere to the discovery of the philosopher Marius Victorinus, which so impressed St. Augustine (*Confessions*, 8, 2, 3–5), that Christianity is not an external institutionalization and organization of ideas or a system of knowledge, but a way that makes a claim on a man, "that he can and must tread" (see *Introduction to Christianity*, pp. 99–100). As a way or a path, not a system or an idea, Christianity becomes recognizable when one enters on it and starts following it (see *Truth and Tolerance*, p. 145).

[33] Ratzinger, *Truth and Tolerance*, p. 142.

[34] Ratzinger, *Pilgrim Fellowship of Faith*, p. 293.

to the gift of the Sacrament, in which the marriage feast of God with mankind is ever and again anticipated".[35]

Individual elements of the Church's mission of journeying with and toward Christ and through him to God include personal and community prayer, celebrating the Eucharist, availing of the sacrament of reconciliation, and obeying the commandments, which enable us to grow in the image of God according to which we are made. The commandments could appear to be no more than a heavy moralistic imposition, were it not for the fact that man's faltering efforts to live in accordance with them are constantly shored up by the grace of forgiveness. In a world filled with darkness and confusion, God has made known to us the way through the gift of his law, while he also shows compassion for us in our weakness and fragility, "time and again picking us up and leading us on".[36] This, as Ratzinger stresses, is a motive for deep joy.

In a world so lacking in joy, Joseph Ratzinger is convinced that the "reawakening of joy in God, joy in God's revelation and in friendship with God" is "an urgent task for the Church in our century".[37] True, the Christian journey is an upward climb, requiring constant purification through the shedding of all that hinders us from drawing close to God, so that we can become capable of the true heights of human existence, of fellowship with God. However, to the extent that we are cleansed, "the climbing, which is at first so difficult, rapidly becomes a joy. This joy must more and more shine forth from the Church into the world." [38]

[35] Ibid., p. 294.
[36] Ibid., p. 297.
[37] Ibid.
[38] Ibid., p. 298.

Chapter IX

EUCHARISTIC JOY

"If we want to understand the Church properly," says Joseph Ratzinger, "then we must look at her ... above all from the standpoint of her liturgy. That is where she is most often herself; that is where she is ever and ever again touched and renewed by the Lord." [1] The Church, as he says elsewhere, "is not merely an external society of believers; by her nature she is a liturgical community; she is most truly Church when she celebrates the Eucharist and makes present the redemptive love of Jesus Christ, which, as love, frees men from their loneliness and leads them to one another by leading them to God." [2] Given this, one would expect a strong connection between joy and the Eucharist, the high point of the Church's liturgy, which is the source and summit of the Christian life. [3]

---

[1] Joseph Ratzinger, *God and the World: A Conversation with Peter Seewald* (San Francisco: Ignatius Press, 2002), p. 343.

[2] Joseph Ratzinger, "The Church as the Sacrament of Salvation", in *Principles of Catholic Theology* (San Francisco: Ignatius Press, 1987), p. 50.

[3] Cf. Second Vatican Council, Constitution on the Sacred Liturgy, *Sacrosanctum Concilium*, December 4, 1963, no. 10.

In his writings, Joseph Ratzinger discusses the various aspects of the Eucharistic mystery: its origins in the Paschal mystery of the Last Supper and the death and Resurrection of Jesus Christ, its sacrificial character, Christ's real Eucharistic presence, Eucharistic adoration, sacramental and spiritual communion, the Eucharist in connection with the Church's mission and social transformation, and the Eucharist as seed of eternal life.[4]

The Eucharist in its various dimensions gives rise to joy: joy for the salvation that the Lord has won for us in the Paschal mystery; joy at the Lord's abiding presence; joy that arises from the intimate union with him that takes place in Eucharistic communion and binds us more closely to the life of the Trinity. Furthermore, the joy that flows from the Eucharist urges us to evangelize and commit ourselves to bringing the "yeast" of the Gospel into society and the world at large. These themes are interconnected, and we can obtain some idea of the richness of Ratzinger's theology of the Eucharist and its connection with Christian joy from a brief examination of what he has to say about Eucharistic sacrifice and presence.

[4] Joseph Ratzinger's more significant contributions include *Eucharistie—Mitte der Kirche* (Munich: Erich Wewel Verlag, 1978); *The Feast of Faith: Approaches to a Theology of the Liturgy* (San Francisco: Ignatius Press, 1986); *A New Song for the Lord: Faith in Christ and the Liturgy* (New York: Crossroad, 1996); *The Spirit of the Liturgy* (San Francisco: Ignatius Press, 2000); "Eucharist and Mission", in *Irish Theological Quarterly* 65 (2000): 245–64; *God Is Near Us: The Eucharist, the Heart of Life* (San Francisco: Ignatius Press, 2003); "Communion: Eucharist-Fellowship-Mission", in *Pilgrim Fellowship of Faith: The Church as Communion* (San Francisco: Ignatius Press, 2005), pp. 60–89; "Eucharist-Communio-Solidarity: Christ Present and Active in the Blessed Sacrament," in *On the Way to Jesus Christ* (San Francisco: Ignatius Press, 2005), pp. 107–28. On Ratzinger's Eucharistic doctrine, see also Stephan Horn, "L'Eucaristia nel concetto di fede di Papa Benedetto XVI", in Congregazione per il Culto Divino e la Disciplina dei Sacramenti, *Redemptionis Sacramentum: L'Eucaristia azione di Cristo e della Chiesa* (Siena: Cantagalli, 2006), pp. 169–86.

Drawing on the teaching of the Council of Trent, the *Catechism of the Catholic Church* explains that the Eucharist is a sacrifice "because it *re-presents* (makes present) the sacrifice of the cross, because it is its *memorial* and because it *applies* its fruits".[5] Joseph Ratzinger presupposes this teaching in discussing the sacrificial character of the Eucharist. In a meditation originally published in *Eucharistie—Mitte der Kirche* in 1978 and reprinted in *God Is Near Us* he draws on the Johannine account of Christ's Passion to establish the connection between the Paschal mystery, the Eucharist, and the life of the Church.[6] This account, as Ratzinger points out, is framed by two moving and theologically significant scenes: the washing of the feet of the disciples (see Jn 13:1–20) and the piercing of Christ's side on the Cross (see Jn 19:31–37). According to the Johannine chronology, Jesus died at exactly the time when the paschal lambs were being sacrificed in the Temple for the feast of Passover. In this way, John wishes to emphasize that Jesus Christ is the true Paschal Lamb. Furthermore, in his account of the piercing of Jesus' side, John employs the Greek word *pleura* ("side"), which was used in the Septuagint version of the creation of Eve from what we usually translate as the "rib" of Adam. John thus makes it clear that Christ "is the new Adam, who goes down into the darkness of death's sleep and opens within it the beginning of a new humanity".[7] From Christ's side, which has been opened up in loving sacrifice, blood and water flow. The early Church Fathers saw in this a symbol of the birth of the Church and of the

---

[5] *Catechism of the Catholic Church*, no. 1366; cf. Council of Trent, Decree on the Most Holy Sacrifice of the Mass, c. 1 (DS 1740).

[6] See Ratzinger, *Eucharistie—Mitte der Kirche*, pp. 21–32, and his *God Is Near Us*, pp. 42–55.

[7] Ratzinger, *God Is Near Us*, p. 43.

fundamental sacraments of baptism and the Eucharist, which continually build up the Church.[8]

Ratzinger insists that the Eucharist is instituted by the Easter mystery as a whole, which embraces Christ's words and gestures at the Last Supper, his death on the Cross, and his Resurrection from the dead. Christ's words are an anticipation of his death: they give his death meaning as a sacrifice of love, making it something that continues to be significant for us. These words carry weight and have creative power for all time because they did not remain mere words but were given content by his actual death. However, they would remain empty claims and unredeemed promises if his love were not shown to be stronger than death. Christ's Resurrection shows that "meaning is stronger than meaninglessness": his love is strong enough to reach out beyond death.[9] Word, death, and Resurrection thus constitute the single mystery of Easter, the Paschal mystery, which is the source and origin of the Eucharist.

The Eucharist, then, is far more than a simple meal, for it has cost a death to provide it. This should give rise to awe and reverence in the presence of the Eucharistic mystery, in which Christ's death becomes a present reality in our midst. However, since the overcoming of Christ's death in his Resurrection is simultaneously present, we can celebrate it as the feast of life and the transformation of the world. Ratzinger, at this point, refers to the common human experience of festival. The ultimate aim of all festivals is, in some way, to open the door of death. As long as it does not touch on the ultimate question of death, a festival remains

[8] On this theme, see Hugo Rahner, *Symbole der Kirche: Die Ekklesiologie der Väter* (Salzburg: Otto Müller Verlag, 1964), pp. 177–205.

[9] Ratzinger, *God Is Near Us*, p. 43.

superficial, a mere form of entertainment to anesthetize oneself. However, there can be no genuine rejoicing or freedom unless this question is addressed. Since the Eucharist provides a definitive response, it is celebratory and joyful in character.[10] It plumbs the depths of death and strikes out on an upward path to life, the life that overcomes death.[11] All of this helps to understand what is meant when we say that the Eucharist is a sacrifice, the "re-presentation", as the Council of Trent puts it, of Christ's sacrifice on the Cross. It is also clear from this that the Eucharist, precisely as sacrifice, is a source of profound joy.

Replying to objections raised against the teaching that the Eucharist is a sacrifice, Ratzinger agrees that God, the giver of all gifts, has no need of our gifts and that man is not an equal partner with God, capable of bartering with him in order to obtain something in return. However, we are indebted to God and, furthermore, we have offended him by our sins. Although we cannot give him anything, we cannot simply assume that he will regard our guilt as being of no consequence. To this dilemma, the Eucharist provides an answer.

The Eucharist teaches us, in the first place, that "*God himself gives to us, that we may give in turn.*"[12] Out of pure love, it is God himself who takes the initiative of reconciling us to himself by giving us his Son as the sacrificial offering by which we may be redeemed. God gives to us in

---

[10] See ibid., p. 44; also ibid., p. 62: "By its being transplanted into the context of the Resurrection, without which the Eucharist would be merely the remembrance of a departure with no return, there arose two natural developments: worship and praise, that it to say, its cultic characteristics, and also joy over the glory of the Risen One."

[11] See ibid., p. 44.

[12] Ibid., p. 45 (author's emphasis).

such a way that we do not remain passive recipients but can give him something. This truth emerges from consideration of Israel's evolving reflection on the nature of sacrifice. As the prophets and Psalms testify, Israel gradually came to the realization that the true sacrifice is the man pleasing to God. Prayer, the grateful praise of God, is the true sacrifice in which we give ourselves back to God, thereby renewing ourselves and the world.[13] This understanding is present in the Haggadah, or prayer of thanksgiving in Israel's Passover, as well as in the Last Supper and in the Christian Eucharist.

By his words, Jesus changed his death into a prayer and, in so doing, transformed the world.[14] As a result, this death is able to be present for us because it lives on in Christ's prayer that continues unceasingly through the centuries. Furthermore, we can share in his death because we can share in his prayer: in this way, we are included in his new and completely efficacious sacrifice, which replaces all the sacrifices of the old dispensation. Jesus Christ is thus present in all ages as the wellspring of life: "He gathers up, so to speak, the pitiful fragments of our suffering, our loving, our hoping, and our waiting into this prayer, into a great flood in which it shares in his life, so that thereby we truly share in the sacrifice."[15]

By cooperating and joining in Christ's sacrifice, our own life, our trials and suffering, our hope and love can become fruitful. Our words can become true worship and sacrifice only when they are given substance by the life and suffering

[13] See ibid. p. 48; also Joseph Ratzinger, *Truth and Tolerance: Christian Belief and World Religions* (San Francisco: Ignatius Press, 2004), p. 149.

[14] See Ratzinger, *God Is Near Us*, p. 49, and his "Form and Content in the Eucharistic Celebration", in *The Feast of Faith*, pp. 33–60.

[15] Ratzinger, *God Is Near Us*, p. 50; cf. ibid., p. 119.

of the Word himself. In the Eucharist, Jesus enables us to pronounce his words with him, thus drawing us into his worship and sacrifice: our words are combined with the Word who ceaselessly gives himself up in love to the Father, and, in this way, the door is opened for us, in death, to resurrection.

As Joseph Ratzinger points out elsewhere, the connection between the Eucharist and the Cross has consequences for our understanding of the Eucharist itself and for our own daily lives as Christians committed to following Christ:

> The Eucharist, as the presence of the cross, is the abiding tree of life, which is ever in our midst and ever invites us to take the fruit of true life.... To receive it, to eat of the tree of life, thus means to receive the crucified Lord and consequently to accept the parameters of his life, his obedience, his "yes," the standard of our creatureliness. It means to accept the love of God, which is our truth—that dependence on God which is no more an imposition from without than is the Son's sonship. It is precisely this dependence that is freedom, because it is truth and love.[16]

The joy of Christians at the Lord's presence in the Eucharist is a recurring theme in Joseph Ratzinger's writings.[17] As he points out, it was joy at God's closeness in the Eucharist that gave rise in the thirteenth century to the Feast of Corpus Christi, which is intended as one great hymn of thanksgiving that such a thing could be. Ratzinger's teachings on Christ's Eucharistic presence draw on the doctrine of the Council of Trent, which affirms that in the most blessed sacrament of the Eucharist "the body and blood,

[16] Joseph Ratzinger, *In the Beginning: A Catholic Understanding of Creation and the Fall* (Grand Rapids: Eerdmans, 1995), pp. 76–77.

[17] On this theme, see especially his meditation "The Presence of the Lord in the Sacrament", in *God Is Near Us*, pp. 74–93.

together with the soul and divinity, of our Lord Jesus Christ and, therefore, the whole Christ is truly, really and substantially present." [18] Christ becomes present in this sacrament when the celebrating priest pronounces the words of Consecration, bringing about the conversion of the bread and wine into Christ's Body and Blood. While the appearances of bread and wine remain, the entire substance or fundamental reality of the bread is converted into Christ's Body and that of the wine is converted into his Blood. However, Christ is present whole and entire in each of the Eucharistic species and in each of their parts. This mysterious conversion, as the Council of Trent teaches, is fittingly and properly termed "transubstantiation". [19]

In John 6, Jesus makes it clear that his Eucharistic presence is to be understood not as a mere figure of speech but quite realistically: "Unless you eat the flesh of the Son of man and drink his blood, you have no life in you. . . . My flesh is food indeed" (Jn 6:53, 55). Christ makes himself present in the Eucharist as food for his disciples; when they eat this food, he takes hold of their bodily existence and unites them to himself. Appealing to the image of the physical union between a man and a woman, St. Paul describes the intensity and reality of this union: "He who is united to the Lord becomes one spirit with him" (1 Cor 6:17). Christ's Eucharistic presence is to be understood as a power that takes hold of us and works to draw us into himself. Unlike other food that is assimilated by the one who eats, the Eucharist brings about a transformation of the one who eats: he is assimilated into Christ

---

[18] Council of Trent, Decree on the Most Holy Eucharist, can. 1 (DS 1651); cf. *Catechism of the Catholic Church*, no. 1374.

[19] See Council of Trent, Decree on the Most Holy Eucharist, c. 3–4 (DS 1641–1642); *Catechism of the Catholic Church*, nos. 1375–77.

and becomes one with him and, through him, with all of Christ's brethren.[20] Receiving Eucharistic Communion brings about a union with Christ that overcomes the limitations imposed by our bodily condition and makes us, with him and on the basis of his Resurrection, capable of resurrection ourselves. In this sense, the Eucharist is a foretaste of eternal life.[21]

Regarding the nature of the change that takes place in the Eucharist, Joseph Ratzinger emphasizes that the Eucharist is to be understood neither as a mere symbol of Christ nor in a crude physical way. Jesus is not present like a piece of meat that can be qualified and quantified.[22] In the Eucharist, what is changed is the substance or the fundamental basis of the being of the species. Although we cannot observe or measure what takes place, since the change is not perceptible to the senses, we know by faith that a real transformation takes place at the deepest level of being: the bread and wine are elevated to a new level of reality in such a way that they become profoundly different, while the appearances of bread and wine remain. The change is in the objective, ontological order: it is not simply a question of putting bread and wine to a new use or merely agreeing that they should indicate some other reality. This is why the Church describes the transformation that takes place in the Eucharist as "transubstantiation", while it regards more recent theories such as "transignification" or "transfinalization", which describe the change merely in terms of a new signification

[20] See Ratzinger, *God Is Near Us*, p. 78; also St. Augustine, *Confessions*, 7, 10, 16: "I am the bread of the strong, eat me! But you will not transform me and make me part of you: rather, I will transform you and make you part of me."

[21] See Ratzinger, *God Is Near Us*, p. 81.

[22] See ibid., p. 85.

or use of the species, as insufficient for an adequate expression of the Eucharistic mystery.[23]

Ratzinger strongly encourages the traditional practice of Eucharistic adoration, a practice made possible by the enduring Eucharistic presence outside of the Mass. Eucharistic adoration is not an optional devotion rendered obsolete by the greater emphasis on the Eucharist as table fellowship and meal, but is vital for more intense personal union with Christ and for the transformation of the world.[24] Communicating with Christ means entering into fellowship with him, and this is not possible without knowing him in a personal relationship that is cultivated through adoration. It must be remembered that the Eucharist is directed to union with the person of Jesus Christ, who is both human and divine. For this reason, we must receive him with an attitude of loving reverence, which recognizes that, while he calls us into a relationship of friendship with him, he remains greater than we are. Eucharistic adoration, "in joy and in hope", involves a two-way dialogue based on the victory of life over death, which enables us to grow in friendship with Christ and to come to a more joyful and more profound inner awareness of the immensity of the gift he offers us.

Sacramental communion is not simply a ritual action performed in common but must also be an intensely personal and spiritual communion with Christ.[25] Prayer in the Lord's

[23] See ibid., pp. 87–88. The most important magisterial evaluation of the theories of transignification and transfinalization is contained in Pope Paul VI's encyclical *Mysterium Fidei*, issued in 1965. While recognizing their positive contribution, the encyclical also indicates their shortcomings and emphasizes the need to maintain the traditional teaching contained in the notion of transubstantiation.

[24] See Ratzinger, *God Is Near Us*, pp. 90, 96, 103, 112, 128.

[25] See ibid., pp. 81–82, 88–93, 102–6.

presence makes reception of the Lord in sacramental communion all the more fruitful. In this regard, we are reminded of St. Augustine's admonition: "No one should eat this flesh without first adoring it.... We should sin were we not to adore it." [26] To reach its full effect and shed its light continually through the day, the Eucharist needs the breath of prayer, "especially in a world that is bored amid the perfection of its occupations, that is not just preoccupied with itself but wishes to be touched by him who alone can give our lives meaning".[27]

Eucharistic adoration also brings about a sensitizing of our conscience, a reinforcement of our moral strength, which is the precondition for every social reform and for every improvement in human affairs.[28] As Ratzinger puts it, "The Lord is near us in our conscience, in his word, in his personal presence in the Eucharist: this constitutes the dignity of the Christian and is the reason for his joy." [29]

Joseph Ratzinger's emphasis on the centrality of the Eucharist as a source of Christian joy has particular consequences for the mission and spirituality of priests. In various writings, he stresses that the priesthood, in all its dimensions, is a continuation of the mission of Christ himself.[30] Priests

[26] St. Augustine, *Enarratio in Psalmum* 98, 9 (CCSL 39: 1385): "nemo autem illam carnem manducat, nisi prius adoraverit ... peccemus non adorando"; cf. Ratzinger, *God Is Near Us*, p. 83; Benedict XVI, Address to the Roman Curia, December 22, 2005, in OR, January 4, 2006, p. 5. On Eucharistic adoration, see Ratzinger, *God Is Near Us*, pp. 88–93, 95–98.

[27] Ratzinger, *God Is Near Us*, p. 128.

[28] See ibid., pp. 98, 105.

[29] Ibid., p. 106.

[30] Apart from Joseph Ratzinger's book *Ministers of Your Joy: Meditations on Priestly Spirituality* (Slough: St. Paul Publications, 1989), other significant contributions include: "Zur Frage nach dem Sinn des priesterlichen Dienstes", in *Geist und Liebe* 41 (1968): 347–76; "Il ministero sacerdotale," in *L'Osservatore*

are to be servants of the Word, the Eucharist, and the Lord's love; in this way, they become "servants of the joy" that will return to them.[31] As ministers of joy, their task is to proclaim the joy of the gospel to the world through word and sacrament, through the witness of their own lives, and through generous openness to all that the Lord asks of them.

In a special way, the priest comes into contact with Christ, the source of his joy, in the daily celebration of the Eucharist. At the school of the Eucharist, we learn how to live correctly. When celebrating the Eucharist, the priest, since he acts *in persona Christi*, is able to speak with the "I" of Christ. To become a priest and to be a priest means constantly to move toward greater identification with Christ; this is the path to God and others, the path of love.[32] Through the dialogue with Christ that takes place in Eucharistic adoration and through the celebration of the Eucharistic sacrifice, the priest experiences and learns to

Romano (Italian-language ed.), May 28, 1970, pp. 3, 8; "The Priest as Mediator and Minister of Christ in the Light of the Message of the New Testament", in *Principles of Catholic Theology*, pp. 267–84; "The Male Priesthood: A Violation of Women's Rights?" in Congregation for the Doctrine of the Faith, *From "Inter Insigniores" to "Ordinatio Sacerdotalis": Documents and Commentaries* (Vatican City: Libreria Editrice Vaticana, 1996), pp. 142–50; "On the Essence of the Priesthood", in *Called to Communion: Understanding the Church Today* (San Francisco: Ignatius Press, 1996), pp. 105–31; "Preparation for Priestly Ministry", in *A New Song for the Lord*, pp. 206–26; "The Ministry and Life of Priests", in *Pilgrim Fellowship of Faith*, pp. 153–75. For a brief overview of Joseph Ratzinger's theology of the priesthood, see Joseph Murphy, "Ministers of Your Joy: Pope Benedict XVI on the Priesthood", in *According to Your Word. Proceedings of a Conference held at the Pontifical Irish College Rome to honour Desmond Cardinal Connell on his Eightieth Birthday*, ed. Liam Bergin (Dublin: Four Courts Press, 2007), pp. 127–42.

[31] Ratzinger, *God Is Near Us*, p. 129. Taking his cue from 2 Cor 1:24, Ratzinger frequently describes priests as servants or ministers of Christian joy, especially in *Ministers of Your Joy*.

[32] See Ratzinger, *A New Song for the Lord*, pp. 225–26.

imitate the self-giving love that has overcome sin and death, making it possible for man to enter into the joy of eternal life.

Consequently, the Eucharist is at the very heart of priestly life. As Pope Benedict exhorted the priests of the diocese of Rome in his first meeting with them, every priest should be able to say in truth: "Holy Mass is the absolute center of my life and of every one of my days." [33] The Eucharist contains in synthetic form the entirety of the priest's mission; since this is so, priests have the great task and responsibility of always living and witnessing "to the mystery that is placed in their hands for the world's salvation". [34]

[33] Benedict XVI, Address to the Clergy of the Diocese of Rome, May 13, 2005, in OR, May 18, 2005, p. 3.
[34] Benedict XVI, Angelus, September 18, 2005, in OR, September 21, 2005, p. 1.

Chapter X

JOY, SUFFERING, AND DEATH

Any attempt to speak about Christian joy must sooner or later face the question of suffering and death. Is it possible to rejoice in the midst of suffering? Can joy be genuine when it is constantly menaced by the fragility of human life and by death itself? Joseph Ratzinger deals with these issues in *Eschatology: Death and Eternal Life*, written for the *Kleine Katholische Dogmatik* series, which he coedited with fellow Regensburg professor Johann Auer. He recalls that suffering and death bring us face to face with the most profound metaphysical questions regarding the meaning and purpose of human existence. All too frequently, however, especially in our modern culture, these are taboo subjects, either repressed or trivialized to avoid facing up to the fundamental questions they pose for our lives. In avoiding them, an opportunity to encounter the truth about ourselves at the profoundest level is missed and, in consequence, it becomes more and more difficult to live a fully human life.[1]

---

[1] See Joseph Ratzinger, *Eschatology: Death and Eternal Life* (Washington, D.C.: Catholic University of America Press, 1988), pp. 69–72.

In the Old Testament, sickness and death are closely associated. Prior to the crisis concerning the traditional wisdom documented in the books of Job and Qoheleth (Ecclesiastes), they are understood as consequences of turning away from God: suffering is a punishment for sin, just as wellbeing is a reward for good deeds.[2] According to the traditional Israelite view of death, the dead man descends into the shadow world of Sheol, a world of nonrelationship where he is cut off from communication with God: God is not in Sheol, nor is he praised there. Sickness too is a realm of non-communication, apparently destroying the relationships that make life what it is, leaving the sick person abandoned and isolated.

While there may be some hint in Job of hope in an abiding life to come (see Job 19:25–27), it is clear that both Job and Qoheleth question the earlier beliefs concerning the destiny of those who have died and the traditional connection between sin and suffering (see Job 9:22–24; Eccl 8:14).[3] In the face of suffering, God seems to be absent: "Behold, I go forward, but he is not there; and backward, but I cannot perceive him; on the left hand I seek him, but I cannot behold him; I turn to the right hand, but I cannot see him" (Job 23:8–9).

The Book of Job, as Ratzinger explains in *God and the World*, "is the classic cry of the man who experiences all the misery of existence and a silent God".[4] Job's questioning shows us how what we do not understand can become the starting point for personal prayer. We too face similar questions: Is it good to be alive? Is God really there? Is he

---

[2] On this, see ibid., pp. 80–92.

[3] See ibid., p. 85.

[4] Joseph Ratzinger, *God and the World: A Conversation with Peter Seewald* (San Francisco: Ignatius Press, 2002), p. 43.

good? Does he help? Unlike Job, Christians pray in the
light of the Paschal mystery of the death and Resurrection
of Jesus, with the underlying certainty that they will get
the right answer, "because he who was crucified, whose
experience was just as miserable and just as dreadful, is always
there before me".[5] In reply to the question of suffering,
there is no clear universal formula, yet the suffering person
who trusts in God knows that God is not silent: he comes
to know something of God's loving presence and compassion, and, realizing that this life is not everything, he places
his hope in the One who raised Jesus from the dead.[6]

In *Eschatology*, Ratzinger goes on to show how the Servant Songs in Deutero-Isaiah, which interpret the painful
experience of the Exile, point to a new level of insight into
the spiritual meaning of suffering and death.[7] In these Songs,
sickness, abandonment, and death are no longer simply punishment for sins but are understood in terms of vicarious
suffering. Through his suffering, God's servant opens the
door of life to others:

> Suffering for God's sake and that of other people can be
> the highest form of allowing God to be present, and plac-
> ing oneself at the service of life.... Sickness and death are
> now the way and the lot of the just wherein justice becomes
> so profound that it turns into the mercy of vicarious service.[8]

Gradually, as Psalms 16 and 73 attest, Israel comes to see
that God is stronger than Sheol, even if explicit belief in

[5] Ibid., p. 42.

[6] On this, see also Joseph Ratzinger, *Der Gott Jesu Christi: Betrachtungen
über den Dreieinigen Gott* (Munich: Kösel, 2006), pp. 74–85.

[7] See Ratzinger, *Eschatology*, p. 86; Joseph Ratzinger, *God Is Near Us: The
Eucharist, the Heart of Life* (San Francisco: Ignatius Press, 2003), pp. 33–34.
The Servant Songs are Is 42:1–9; 49:1–6; 50:4–11; 52:13–53:12.

[8] Ratzinger, *Eschatology*, pp. 86–87.

the Resurrection is not immediately affirmed. Psalm 73 is particularly significant.[9] Having recognized the transient quality of the happiness of the wicked, the psalmist, although he does not offer a theory of immortality, discovers that communion with God is the true reality: "I am continually with you; you hold my right hand. You guide me with your counsel, and afterward you will receive me to glory. Whom have I in heaven but you? And there is nothing upon earth that I desire besides you" (vv. 23–25). In comparison, everything else, no matter how massively it exerts itself, is nothing. Being with God is seen as the point from which the ever-present and all-devouring menace of Sheol may be overcome:

> My flesh and my heart may fail, but God is the strength of my heart and my portion for ever. For behold, those who are far from you shall perish; you put an end to those who are false to you. But for me it is good to be near God; I have made the Lord GOD my refuge, that I may tell of all your works (vv. 26–28).

Finally, the later Old Testament writings, such as Daniel, Wisdom, and the two books of the Maccabees, testify to a new understanding of death and the afterlife. Daniel 12:2 is the clearest formulation of resurrection faith that the Old Testament contains: "Many of those who sleep in the dust of the earth shall awake, some to everlasting life, and some to shame and everlasting contempt." Martyrdom raises new questions regarding the connection between sin and death, for it is not because he sins but precisely because he professes belief in God that the martyr is put to death. The believer comes to recognize that the man who dies in God's

[9] See Ratzinger's commentary on this psalm in ibid., pp. 88–90; also in Ratzinger, *God Is Near Us*, pp. 137–40.

righteousness does not disappear into nothingness but enters the authentic reality of life itself.[10] The Book of Wisdom contains fundamentally the same spirituality of suffering and martyrdom. This kind of spirituality is highly realistic, since it enables one to discern what is of lasting worth and to give priority in all things to God, the source of all life.

With this we come to the New Testament. While the main ideas concerning suffering and death are already present in the Old Testament, we now encounter something radically new: the fact of the martyrdom of Jesus Christ, the Just One, and his Resurrection.

God's saving work, accomplished through Christ's Passion, death, and Resurrection, sheds new light on the whole question of suffering. At the Last Supper, through the words of institution, Christ "transforms death into the spiritual act of affirmation, into the act of self-sharing love, into the act of adoration, which is offered to God, then from God is made available to men".[11] By transforming death into an act of love and truth, Christ establishes the definitive covenant between God and man and gives us access to new life. God's saving work is achieved through the Cross, which is the characteristic sign of the paradoxical manner in which God brings about his success.

As Ratzinger says, what strengthens our faith is not the Church of people who are successful or powerful in human terms, but the Church of the suffering. This Church, the Church of the martyrs, is the permanent sign that God exists and that man, far from being something to be discarded, is capable of being saved.[12] The Church of the suffering is a

---

[10] See Ratzinger, *Eschatology*, p. 91.

[11] Ratzinger, *God Is Near Us*, p. 29.

[12] See ibid., p. 40.

sign that gives us hope and courage, purifying us and opening our hearts to God's way of operating in the world.

Given this, we can understand the New Testament's teaching that Christ's victory, without playing down or denying
the reality of suffering, makes it possible for joy and suffering to coexist.[13] St. Paul speaks of his own joy in the midst
of suffering (see Phil 1:3–26; 2 Cor 6:10), and he encourages the various Christian communities to whom he writes
not to be anxious but to rejoice in the Lord always (see 1
Thess 5:16–18; Phil 3:1; 4:4). In addition, suffering plays
no small part in the experience of the author of the First
Letter of St. Peter, who exhorts Christians in the northern
part of Asia Minor to remain steadfast in faith and indeed
to rejoice despite their trials.[14] They are to contemplate
the example of Christ, who obtained joy for himself as well
as for others through his death and Resurrection. The future
inheritance laid up for them in heaven can bring joy in the
present world, while what they now have to endure is a
means of probation (see 1 Pet 1:6–7). Although they cannot see Christ now, his disciples love him, believe in him,
and "rejoice with unutterable and exalted joy" (1 Pet 1:8).
They are not to be afraid: those who have to suffer for the
sake of righteousness are blessed (see 1 Pet 3:14; also Mt
5:10). Their trials are a sharing in Christ's sufferings and
should be a cause for rejoicing: "If you are reproached for
the name of Christ, you are blessed, because the spirit of
glory and of God rests upon you" (1 Pet 4:14). It is clear,

[13] On this theme, see Hans Urs von Balthasar, "Joy and the Cross", in
Truth is Symphonic: Aspects of Christian Pluralism (San Francisco: Ignatius Press,
1987), pp. 152–69; Janez Zupet, "Attraverso la croce la gioia è venuta nel
mondo", in *Communio* (Italian-language edition) 195 (2004): 8–17.

[14] On this, see William G. Morrice, *Joy in the New Testament* (Exeter: The
Paternoster Press, 1984), pp. 138–41.

then, that Christian joy is founded on eschatological hope, since suffering for Christ's sake brings the reward of eternal happiness, and on the blessing of the Holy Spirit's presence.

In *The Yes of Jesus Christ*, Ratzinger addresses the question of whether it is possible to rejoice in the midst of suffering. Referring to the Sermon on the Mount, he describes the beatitudes as an expression of the paradox and tension at the heart of Christian living, citing as an example the beatitude "Blessed are those who mourn, for they shall be comforted" (Mt 5:4).[15] Those who suffer or mourn are in reality blessed because God is close to them, is concerned about them, and will in the future make his presence known. Hence, in their distress, they are not to fear. St. Paul illustrates the paradox of Christian living in his own life, especially as he recounts it in the Second Letter to the Corinthians (see 4:16–18; 6:8b–10), where among other things he describes God's ministers and thus himself "as sorrowful, yet always rejoicing" (6:10). Christian life is characterized by the paradox of hope: "Dying, and behold we live" (6:9; see 4:7–12). Christ invites us to follow him in discipleship and, as our relationship with him deepens, we are internally renewed (see 4:16). As members of Christ's body, we should place our trust in him, who is our hope, the anchor of our lives.

Ratzinger acknowledges that the various difficulties of life could tempt us not to believe in God's love and, in consequence, to revolt against him.[16] Unfortunately, those who rebel in this way end up poisoning their own lives. God, however, calls us to trust in him. By doing so, we

---

[15] See Joseph Ratzinger, *The Yes of Jesus Christ: Exercises in Faith, Hope and Love* (New York: Crossroad, 2005), pp. 56–58.

[16] See ibid., p. 111.

discover that, despite whatever sufferings and trials we may have to face, his love is always present and he has, in fact, been quietly working for our good. In this regard, there are many examples of people who have dared to place their trust in God and, as a result, have discovered true happiness precisely in what seemed to be their greatest hour of darkness. All of this shows that inner agreement with God belongs to the happy life. Only when this fundamental relationship is in order can all other relationships be right. Love grows from a right relationship with God based on assent, trust, and agreement, and it flows out into love of neighbor.

How then is death to be understood? Both the Old and the New Testaments see it as something contrary to God. Like all that is opposed to God, death too is destined to be overcome, to be cast into the lake of fire and to be destroyed (see Rev 20:14; 1 Cor 15:26). At the same time, Jesus Christ underwent suffering and abandonment even unto death. The Just One descended into Sheol, where the praise of God is never heard. As a result of his descent,

> death ceases to be the God-forsaken land of darkness, a realm of unpitying distance from God. In Christ, God himself entered that realm of death, transforming the space of non-communication into the place of his own presence. This is no apotheosis of death. Instead, God has cancelled out and overcome death in entering it through Christ.[17]

The Christian message of the Cross enables us to enter more deeply into the mystery of life and death. Dying is not just the ending of our biological existence. It is present in the lack of authenticity, closedness, and emptiness that too often characterize our daily lives. In fact, says Ratzinger,

---

[17] Ratzinger, *Eschatology*, p. 93 (slightly modified).

our lives are less threatened by the physical pain and disease heralding the onset of death than by the failure to be at one with our true being, a failure that allows the promise of life to evaporate, leaving only banalities and leading to final emptiness.[18] The complex phenomenon of death manifests itself in various related ways:

> Firstly, death is present as the nothingness of an empty existence which ends up in a mere semblance of living. Secondly, death is present as the physical process of disintegration which accompanies life. It is felt in sickness, and reaches its terminal point in physical dying. Thirdly, death is met with in the daring of that love which leaves self behind, giving itself to the other. It is likewise encountered in the abandonment of one's own advantage for the sake of justice and truth.[19]

Pain and disease have the effect of shattering one physically, psychologically, and spiritually. However, they can also help a person to overcome complacency and spiritual lethargy. Suffering teaches that life is not completely at our disposal. We could try to avoid facing up to this truth and adopt an attitude of anger or resentment toward the limitations that suffering imposes on our capacity to act for ourselves. Alternatively, we could respond positively by placing our trust in the strange power to which we are subject, a power that Christians know to be God. In so doing, our acceptance of pain and suffering becomes an act of confidence, trust, and love. The experience of suffering and the prospect of physical death force us to make a choice between what Ratzinger calls the "pattern of love", characterized by acceptance of our real condition and loving confidence in

[18] See ibid., p. 95.
[19] Ibid.

God, or the "pattern of power", that involves a desperate, angry, and ultimately futile attempt to maintain complete autonomous control over our life and destiny.[20]

The Cross of Christ comes to our assistance here, for it reveals that God personally fulfilled the pattern of love beyond all expectations and, in so doing, justified that human confidence which is ultimately the only alternative to self-destruction.[21] The Christian does not die alone; he dies into the death of Jesus Christ himself. He knows he has been created for love and can place his confidence in the supreme love that has removed the sting of death. Rather than escaping death or hoping that it will catch him unawares, the Christian accepts death and the challenges of the metaphysical questions it poses. In facing death time and time again throughout life, he matures for the real life, which is eternal.

All of this brings us back to the question of truth. The Christian shares in the life and death of Christ, not so much by any spectacular gesture as by the daily readiness to give greater weight to faith, to truth, and to what is right. It is only possible for us to place our confidence in truth when we are convinced that truth exists and has made itself known to us. Martyrdom with Christ, the repeated act of giving truth more importance than self, is nothing other than the movement of love itself, a movement that faith makes possible. Attempts to construct our own lives in a self-sufficient manner, which at bottom represent subtle and often unconscious attempts to ensure that we survive in some fashion after death, if only in the memory of others, are ultimately doomed to failure. However, when we cease to try to build

[20] See ibid., p. 96.
[21] See ibid., p. 97.

our lives according to our own little plans and instead surrender ourselves to truth, to love, and to what is right, we
discover true life, which is Christ's gift to us.[22]

These considerations shed further light on the meaning
of suffering. While Christians do not deliberately seek out
suffering, they know that without the Passion man does
not reach the hidden depths of life and consequently fails
to attain genuine fulfillment. For this reason, Christian faith
rejects as contrary to human nature any attempt to avoid
suffering through some form of Stoic *apatheia* or Epicurean
enjoyment that would cast out pain as alien or simply bracket
it out. Such approaches deny the truth of man and preclude his reaching true greatness of life. Christ did not emu-
late the noble detachment of the philosopher Socrates in
the face of death, but experienced the abandonment and
isolation of death in all its horror, accepting the cup of
being human down to its last dregs. While it is legitimate
to try to reduce suffering in various ways, through medi-
cine, psychology, education, or the building of a new society, its complete abolition would cause man no longer to
face up to life. To act against the Cross is to act against the
truth. Ratzinger concludes: "The only sufficient answer to
the question of man is a response which discharges the infinite claims of love. Only eternal life corresponds to the
question raised by human living and dying on this earth." [23]

---

[22] See ibid., pp. 99–100.

[23] Ibid., p. 103. For a more recent discussion on suffering, which further
develops the insights presented in this chapter, see Benedict XVI, Encyclical
Letter *Spe Salvi*, November 30, 2007, nn. 36–40 (Vatican City: Libreria Editrice Vaticana, 2007).

Chapter XI

ETERNAL JOY

Sunday after Sunday, in the Church's liturgy, we recite the Creed, in which we profess: "We look for the resurrection of the dead and the life of the world to come." This article of faith has, however, come to sound quite foreign to many, impinging little on their daily lives. Rather than finding belief in eternal life consoling, it seems nebulous and unreal, perhaps not even worth striving for.

Describing this situation, Hans Urs von Balthasar opined: "It is as if modern man had a tendon cut, so that he can no longer run toward his original goal, as if his wings had been clipped, as if his spiritual awareness of transcendence had withered." [1] Of course, the idea of some kind of life after death has not completely disappeared—after all, it is present in some form or other in the various world religions. However, it often manifests itself today in a vague belief in some kind of reincarnated existence.

Joseph Ratzinger discusses this problem in a lecture first given to the Christian Academy in Prague in 1992 and

[1] Hans Urs von Balthasar, "Der Mensch und das ewige Leben", in *Internationale katholische Zeitschrift Communio* 20 (1991): 3.

subsequently published in *God Is Near Us*.[2] In it, he connects modern man's lack of awareness of eternal life in
part with our inability to imagine what eternal life might
be and in part with the all too prevalent difficulty in believ-
ing that God really does intervene in the world, a difficulty that is all too evident in the widespread tendency to
play down the reality of the miracles of the New Testament, the Virgin Birth, and Christ's Resurrection from the
dead. Many are of the view that, once created, the world
is a closed system and all that happens in it can be explained
only in terms of the natural laws that govern this world.
On this reading, God is no longer an active agent in history.

It is clear then that the withering of hope in eternity is
intimately connected with the withering of faith in the living God, who is Trinity, the God of love, the Creator, and
the Redeemer.[3] Belief in eternal life can revive only if we
discover a new relationship with God that sees him as active
in the world and in our regard: "We simply have to become
once more aware of the living God and of his love. Then
we will know that this love, which is eternal and is a great
power, will not abandon us."[4]

The promise of eternal life is the response to man's deep-
seated desire for justice, truth, love, and happiness. Eternal
life is not a matter of living a long time but denotes a certain quality of existence, characterized by justice, truth, and
love, in which duration as an endless sequence of moments
disappears. On this understanding, eternal life would be a
punishment for anyone who is so identified with injustice,

[2] Joseph Ratzinger, "My Joy is to Be in Thy Presence: On the Christian
Belief in Eternal Life", in *God Is Near Us: The Eucharist, the Heart of Life* (San
Francisco: Ignatius Press, 2003), pp. 130–48.

[3] See ibid., p. 132.

[4] Ibid., p. 134.

lies, and hatred that the coming of justice, truth, and love would be a negation of his entire existence. Such an existence would have to be described as damnation, and it is in this that hell essentially consists.[5]

Eternal life "is not an endless series of moments, in which we would have to try to overcome boredom and anxiety in the face of what cannot be ended."[6] It is a new quality of life, freed from the fragmentation of existence in the accelerating flight of moments, in which everything flows into the eternal "now" of love. Hence, eternal life is not something completely beyond our understanding or imagination or something reserved for the world to come. As a new quality of existence it can be present to some extent in this life: it describes what happens when we encounter Christ, an encounter that is already present in this life in its fundamental elements.[7] The eternal life of heaven means coming to know more deeply and definitively God's hidden presence, by whose gift we truly live.[8]

Illustrating the point by reference to Psalm 73, Ratzinger explains that eternal life is present wherever we come face to face with God: "Like a great love, it can no longer be taken from us by any change or chance; rather, it is an indestructible heart from which spring the courage and the joy to go on, even when exterior things are painful and hard."[9] God helps man to see things in perspective, to understand where true riches are to be found. In his contact with God, man comes to see that true life, which is everything,

[5] See ibid., p. 136.

[6] Ibid., p. 137.

[7] See Joseph Ratzinger, *Eschatology: Death and Eternal Life* (Washington, D.C.: Catholic University of America Press, 1988), p. 233.

[8] See ibid., p. 234.

[9] Ratzinger, *God Is Near Us*, p. 137.

has been granted to him and that his joy is to be in God's presence (cf. Ps 73:25–28). Eternal life thus involves living a certain quality of life in our present existence. If we live in this way, then the hope of eternal fellowship with God "will become the expectation that characterizes our existence, because some conception of its reality develops for us, and the beauty of it transforms us from within".[10]

From this it is clear that eternal life also has a significant ecclesiological dimension. It is not a private, individualistic affair, but implies fellowship with all who have been accepted by God's love: "Because we all share in God's love, we belong to each other." [11] As members of the body of Christ, the joys of one are the joys of all, and the sufferings of one are the sufferings of all.

Given this understanding of eternal life, it is clear that the present and eternity are not juxtaposed but interwoven. In this lies the difference between eschatology and utopia.[12] For a long time, utopia with its hope of a better world in the future, whether of the Marxist or liberal variety, has been offered in place of eternal life, which is supposedly unreal and said to alienate us from real time. Utopia, with its concomitant myth of the ideal future society to be brought about by man's efforts alone, without faith in God, is a deception that leads to the destruction of our hopes. Rather than striving for an impossible utopia, we should instead devote our efforts to strengthen those factors that hold evil at bay in the present and that can, therefore, offer some hope for the immediate future. According to Ratzinger, our

[10] Ibid., pp. 140–41.

[11] Ibid., p. 141.

[12] On this, see also Joseph Ratzinger, "Eschatology and Utopia", in *Church, Ecumenism and Politics: New Essays in Ecclesiology* (Slough: St. Paul Publications, 1988), pp. 237–54.

task is "to preserve anything good that has already been achieved, to overcome anything bad that exists at the time, and to guard against the outbreak of destructive forces".[13] This requires striving to do God's will and praying for his help. In doing so, "truth springs up, justice arises, love comes to be".[14] This irruption of eternity in the present is what brings about the Kingdom of God, which is always closer than any imaginary utopia because it can always take up time within itself and make of it pure presence. God's kingdom is not only a future reality but is also truly present wherever the Lord brings us together in his body and places our will within the divine will.

Life shared with God or eternal life within temporal life is possible because God lives with us: "Christ is God being here with us." [15] God is not a distant God whom no bridge can reach; rather, he is at hand: the body of the Son is the bridge for our souls. As part of the body of the Son, every single person's relationship with God has been blended together in the Son's one relationship with God. God is not simply a God "up there", but, because he has descended to the very depths of the earth (cf. Eph 4:9f.), he surrounds us on all sides; he is all in all and so all belongs to him. What began with Christ's renunciation on the Cross of what was properly his will be complete when the Son finally hands over to the Father the kingdom, "that is, ingathered humanity and the creation that is carried with them (1 Cor 15:28)".[16]

Hence, the purely private existence of the isolated self no longer exists, but "all that is mine is yours" (Lk 15:31).

[13] Joseph Ratzinger, *Truth and Tolerance: Christian Belief and World Religions* (San Francisco: Ignatius Press, 2004), p. 257.

[14] Ratzinger, *God Is Near Us*, p. 143.

[15] Ibid., p. 144.

[16] Ibid., p. 145.

In the body of Christ, each member lives for every other one: each accepted suffering or pain, every act of love or renunciation, every turning to God, becomes effective for all. Nothing that is good goes to waste:

> Against the power of evil, whose tentacles threaten to sur-
> round and lay hold of every part of our society, to choke it in
> their deadly embrace, this quiet cycle of true life appears as
> the liberating force by which the Kingdom of God, without
> any abolition of what is existing, is, as the Lord says, already
> in the midst of us (Lk 17:21). Within this cycle God's King-
> dom comes, because God's will is done on earth as in heaven.[17]

All of this outlines the main features of what is understood by "heaven" and "hell". Similarly, the ultimate reality behind the "place of purification", or "purgatory", is
Christ himself.[18] When we face him without disguise, then
all that is wretched and guilty in our lives will stand in
that moment of truth before our souls in flames of fire.
Encounter with the Lord burns away our dross and refashions
us to be vessels of eternal joy.[19] The effect of the Lord's
presence is that everything within us that is contradictory
to eternal life, to Christ's love, that is, everything that is
interwoven with injustice, hatred, or lies, will be burnt
away in a process of purification.

Similarly, Christ is the judgment. In encountering him,
all that is base, twisted, and sinful in our existence will be
exposed; we have to be freed from these in the pain of
purification. Ratzinger, following Romano Guardini and
Hans Urs von Balthasar, adds that the judgment will also

[17] Ibid.
[18] Ratzinger traces the history and presents a Christological interpretation
of the essential core of the doctrine of purgatory in *Eschatology*, pp. 218–33.
[19] See ibid., p. 231.

be the moment when we will understand why creation exists, why all the incomprehensible things have arisen in it as a result of our freedom to do evil. In response to our questions, "the Lord will show us his wounds, and we will understand." [20] In the meantime, we are to trust in him and believe what these wounds tell us, even though we cannot work right through the logic of this world.

In conclusion, then, eternal life or heaven is not something foreign to this life. It is a veiled reality now present and awaiting perfect fulfillment. One is in heaven when and to the degree that one is in Christ. Since the glorified Christ is in a constant attitude of self-giving to the Father, heaven, as our becoming one with Christ, takes on the nature of adoration. All our earthly worship prefigures it and in it comes to completion. In Christ, who is the "cultic space for God", the ascending movement of humanity meets the descending movement of God in his self-gift to us. Hence, worship in its heavenly perfected form entails an immediacy between God and man that knows no setting asunder. In heaven, God is "all in all" and thus the human person enters upon his boundless fulfillment. [21]

Oneness with Christ also means oneness with all who are members of his body. Thus, heaven is a stranger to isolation. As the society of the communion of saints, of all who have opened themselves up in love to God and to one another, it is the fulfillment of all human communion. [22] The communion of the whole body of Christ is not ruptured: there is a closeness of love that knows no limit and is sure of attaining God in our neighbor and our neighbor in God.

[20] Ratzinger, *God Is Near Us*, p. 147.

[21] See Ratzinger, *Eschatology*, pp. 234–35.

[22] See ibid., p. 235.

Heaven is in itself eschatological reality. Its definitive character arises from the definitiveness of God's irrevocable love. Heaven will be complete when all the members of the Lord's body are gathered in: such completion involves the resurrection of the flesh and the Parousia, when the presence of Christ, so far only inaugurated among us, will reach its fullness and encompass all who are to be saved and the entire cosmos with them. Explaining that heaven comes in two stages, Ratzinger synthesizes his teaching on heaven, emphasizing its Christocentric character, its individual and interpersonal dimensions and its joyfulness:

> The Lord's exaltation gives rise to the new unity of God with man, and hence to heaven. The perfecting of the Lord's body in the *plērōma* of the "whole Christ" brings heaven to its true cosmic completion. Let us say it once more before we end: the individual's salvation is whole and entire only when the salvation of the cosmos and all the elect has come to full fruition. For the redeemed are not simply adjacent to each other in heaven. Rather, in their being together as the one Christ, they *are* heaven. In that moment, the whole creation will become song. It will be a single act in which, forgetful of self, the individual will break through the limits of being into the whole, and the whole takes up its dwelling in the individual. It will be joy in which all questioning is resolved and satisfied.[23]

Joy, which is a gift of Trinitarian love, is made perfect when God becomes "all in all" and we are definitively united with him in the adoring and rejoicing communion of heaven, which is already a hidden reality in this life.

---

[23] Ibid., p. 238. On the themes discussed in this chapter, see also Benedict XVI, Encyclical Letter *Spe Salvi*, November 30, 2007, nn. 41–48 (Vatican City: Libreria Editrice Vaticana, 2007).

CONCLUSION

Christianity is a religion of joy; it is truly "gospel", or "glad tidings", for mankind. This is the testimony of the entirety of Scripture and especially of the New Testament, which really begins with the angel's greeting to Mary: "Rejoice!" (Lk 1:28).[1]

The conviction that Christ is our true joy and that living the Christian faith to the full gives rise to joy has always accompanied the present Holy Father, as is clear from an Advent meditation, originally published in 1958, in which he comments on St. Paul's exhortation to rejoice in the Lord always (see Phil 4:4):

> The concept of joy is really a fundamental one for Christianity, which essentially is and seeks to be "*evangelium*", glad tidings. Yet, the world has lost faith in the Gospel, in Christ, and forsakes the Church for the sake of the joy which, it is said, would be denied to man by Christianity, with all its endless prescriptions and prohibitions. Certainly, it is true that the joy of Christ is not as easy to find as the banal pleasure that arises from any kind of amusement. It would be mistaken, however, to interpret the words "Rejoice in the Lord" as if they meant: "Rejoice, *but* in the Lord", as if the second phrase revoked what was said in the first. The Apostle simply says: "Rejoice in the Lord", because he clearly believes that every true joy is contained in the Lord and that outside of him there is no true joy. Indeed, it is also just as true that

[1] See Joseph Ratzinger, "Faith as Trust and Joy—Evangelium", in *Principles of Catholic Theology* (San Francisco: Ignatius Press, 1987), p. 75.

every joy found independently of him or in opposition to
him fails to satisfy, but continually causes a person such agi-
tation that, in the end, he can really no longer be joyful.
Thus, we need to have it said to us that only with Christ has
true joy made its appearance and that, in our own lives, nothing matters apart from learning to see and understand Christ,
the God of grace, the light and joy of the world. Indeed,
our joy will only be true if it is not based on things, which
can be taken away from us and destroyed, but thrusts its roots
into the intimate depth of our lives, into that depth which
no worldly power can take away from us. In addition, every
external loss should become for us an initiation into that
interiority and should make us more mature for living our
true life.[2]

During his meeting with the clergy of the diocese of
Aosta in July 2005, Pope Benedict XVI provided a brief
summary of his teaching on joy, distinguishing it from mere
pleasure and drawing attention to its connection with love
and the possibility of its maturing through suffering:

It must be made clear that pleasure is not everything, that
Christianity gives us joy, just as love gives us joy. But love
is also always a renunciation of self. The Lord himself has
given us the formula of what love is: he who loses himself
finds himself; he who spares or saves himself is lost. It is
always an "Exodus", and therefore it always entails suffering. True joy is something different from pleasure: joy grows
and continues to mature in suffering in communion with

[2] Joseph Ratzinger, "Vom Sinn des Advents", in his *Wer hilft uns leben?
Von Gott und Mensch*, ed. Holger Zaborowski and Alwin Letzkus (Freiburg
im Breisgau: Herder, 2005), pp. 104–5. This meditation was originally published under the same title in *Klerusblatt* (München) 38 (1958): 418–20 and
subsequently reprinted in *Dogma und Verkündigung* (Munich and Freiburg in
Breisgau: Erich Wewel Verlag, 1973), pp. 373–82.

the Cross of Christ. It is here alone that the true joy of faith is born.[3]

Joy, as Pope Benedict constantly emphasizes, presupposes goodness, love, and truth: it arises from the love that is absolutely true and unfailing, namely, God's love for men. Recovery of an authentic sense of Christian joy, which is solidly rooted in the objective truth that God reveals about man and his destiny and in God's love that ever accompanies us, is urgent in order to overcome the boredom, spiritual lethargy, and corrosive sense of meaninglessness that afflict so many of our contemporaries. By discovering the joy that comes from knowing God's love and their great calling will they see life as having meaning and direction, as something worth living.

Through fidelity to the truth and by living in accordance with the theological virtues of faith, hope, and charity, we experience in our own lives the joy that comes from God. By growing in the Christian life according to the inner dynamism of the theological virtues, our joy in the Lord increases and enables us to face all situations with serene confidence in God, who is always at hand to lead and assist us.

Christian joy is God's gift, rooted in the love of the Triune God, which is the model and source of all true love. Far from being the product of mere chance, every man and woman is brought into existence by God in accordance with a loving plan. While sin damages our relations with God and with one another, he does not abandon us but sends his Son to save us. He also bestows on us the gift of the Holy Spirit, whose inner presence brings joy to the heart

[3] Benedict XVI, Meeting with the Clergy of the Diocese of Aosta, July 25, 2005, in OR, August 3, 2005, p. 5 (translation corrected).

of man, in order to make us holy and to lead us into the fullness of truth.

The Church, built up through the Eucharist and guided by the Holy Spirit, has the mission of maintaining this spirit of joy in the world, by making God's love known through the celebration of the sacraments, the teaching of the one truth that saves and the example of charity to all. At the heart of the Church is Christ's Eucharistic presence, a gift that enables us to share in Christ's saving work and experience the ineffable joy of a close relationship with him.

Perseverance in Christian living enables us to face sickness and suffering as privileged and even joyful encounters with God's love and to understand death not as the definitive separation from all we love but as the gateway to true life. Indeed, eternal life itself is not something restricted to the next life, but begins now, wherever people live in accordance with justice, truth, and love.

The message of joy, which is at the heart of Christianity, is a message about meaning and about love: man's life has meaning because he is loved by the one love that can never fail. The world, today, as in the past, is in urgent need of hearing this message:

> We have a new need for that primordial trust which ultimately only faith can give. That the world is basically good, that God is there and is good. That it is good to live and be a human being. This results, then, in the courage to rejoice, which in turn becomes commitment to making sure that other people, too, can rejoice and receive good news.[4]

[4] Joseph Ratzinger, *Salt of the Earth: Christianity and the Catholic Church at the End of the Millennium, An Interview with Peter Seewald* (San Francisco: Ignatius Press, 1997), p. 37.

BIBLIOGRAPHY

For a bibliography of Joseph Ratzinger's works, as of February 1, 2002, see his *Pilgrim Fellowship of Faith: The Church as Communion* (San Francisco: Ignatius Press, 2005), pp. 299–379. The bibliography that follows lists works mentioned in this book, according to the date of first publication. English translations (ET), where they exist, are noted in all cases, even if not used in this book.

WORKS OF JOSEPH RATZINGER

Volk und Haus Gottes in Augustins Lehre von der Kirche. Munich: Zink, 1954. Unamended reprint, with a new preface: St. Ottilien: EOS Verlag, 1992. No English translation.

"Vom Sinn des Advents". In *Klerusblatt* (München) 38 (1958): 418–20. Reprinted in his *Dogma und Verkündigung*. Munich and Freiburg in Breisgau: Erich Wewel Verlag, 1973, pp. 373–82. Also in *Wer hilft uns leben? Von Gott und Mensch*. Edited by Holger Zaborowski and Alwin Letzkus. Freiburg im Breisgau: Herder, 2005, pp. 96–106.

Die Geschichtstheologie des heiligen Bonaventura. Munich: Schnell und Steiner, 1959. Unamended reprint, with a new preface: St. Ottilien: EOS Verlag, 1992. ET: *The Theology of History in St. Bonaventure*. Chicago: Franciscan Herald Press, 1971.

"Stellvertretung". In *Handbuch Theologischer Grundbegriffe*. Edited by Heinrich Fries. Vol. 2. Munich: Kösel, 1963, pp. 566–75. No English translation.

Vom Sinn des Christseins: Drei Adventspredigten. Munich: Kösel, 1965; 2nd ed., 2005. ET: *What It Means to Be a Christian.* San Francisco: Ignatius Press, 2006.

Theological Highlights of Vatican II. New York: Paulist Press, 1966. This volume contains the English translation of the four brief commentaries that Joseph Ratzinger wrote every year on the various sessions of the Second Vatican Council: *Die erste Sitzungsperiode des 2. Vatikanischen Konzils: Ein Rückblick.* Cologne: Bachem, 1963; *Das Konzil auf dem Weg: Rückblick auf die zweite Sitzungsperiode.* Cologne: Bachem, 1964; *Ergebnisse und Probleme der dritten Konzilsperiode.* Cologne: Bachem, 1965; *Die letzte Sitzungsperiode des Konzils.* Cologne: Bachem, 1966.

"Zum Personverständnis in der Dogmatik". In *Das Personverständnis in der Pädagogik und ihren Nachbarwissenschaften.* Edited by Josef Speck. Münster: A. Henn Verlag, 1966, pp. 157–71. ET: "Concerning the Notion of Person in Theology". In *Communio* (American ed.) 17 (1990): 439–54.

Einführung in das Christentum: Vorlesungen über das Apostolische Glaubensbekenntnis. Munich: Kösel, 1968. New edition, unamended but with a new introduction: Munich: Kösel, 2000. ET: *Introduction to Christianity.* 2nd ed., San Francisco: Ignatius Press, 2004.

"Zur Frage nach dem Sinn des priesterlichen Dienstes". In *Geist und Liebe* 41 (1968): 347–76.

Das Neue Volk Gottes: Entwürfe zur Ekklesiologie. Düsseldorf: Patmos, 1969. No English translation.

"Il ministero sacerdotale". In *L'Osservatore Romano* (daily Italian-language ed.), May 28, 1970, pp. 3, 8.

Dogma und Verkündigung. Munich and Freiburg im Breisgau: Erich Wewel Verlag, 1973. ET (partial): *Dogma and Preaching.* Chicago: Franciscan Herald Press, 1985.

"Vorfragen zu einer Theologie der Erlösung". In *Erlösung und Emanzipation*. Edited by Leo Scheffczyk. Freiburg: Herder, 1973, pp. 141–55. No English translation.

Die Hoffnung des Senfkorns. Meitingen and Freising: Kyrios Verlag, 1973. No English translation.

"Kirchliches Lehramt—Glaube—Moral". In *Prinzipien christlicher Moral*. Edited together with Heinrich Schürmann and Hans Urs von Balthasar. Einsiedeln: Johannes Verlag, 1975. ET: "The Church's Teaching Authority—Faith—Morals". In *Principles of Christian Morality*. San Francisco: Ignatius Press, 1986.

Der Gott Jesu Christi: Betrachtungen über den Dreienigen Gott. Munich: Kösel, 1976; new ed., 2006. ET: *The God of Jesus Christ: Meditations on God in the Trinity*. Chicago: Franciscan Herald Press, 1978.

"Il sacerdozio dell'uomo: un'offesa ai diritti della donna?" In *L'Osservatore Romano* (daily Italian-language ed.), March 26, 1977, pp. 1–2. ET: "The Male Priesthood: A Violation of Women's Rights?" In Congregation for the Doctrine of the Faith, *From "Inter Insigniores" to "Ordinatio Sacerdotalis": Documents and Commentaries*. Vatican City: Libreria Editrice Vaticana, 1996, pp. 142–50.

Eschatologie—Tod und ewiges Leben. Regensburg: Pustet, 1977; 6th enlarged ed., 1990. ET: *Eschatology: Death and Eternal Life*. Washington, D.C.: Catholic University of America Press, 1988.

Die Tochter Zion: Betrachtungen über den Marienglauben der Kirche. Einsiedeln: Johannes Verlag, 1977; 4th ed., 1990. ET: *Daughter Zion: Meditations on the Church's Marian Belief*. San Francisco: Ignatius Press, 1983.

"Alcune forme bibliche ed ecclesiali di 'presenza' dello Spirito nella storia". In *Spirito Santo e storia*. Edited by L. Sartori. Rome: Ave, 1977, pp. 51–64.

Eucharistie—Mitte der Kirche. Munich: Erich Wewel Verlag, 1978. ET: *God Is Near Us: The Eucharist, the Heart of Life.* San Francisco: Ignatius Press, 2003, pp. 27–93.

Maria—Kirche im Ursprung. With Hans Urs von Balthasar. Freiburg im Breisgau: Herder, 1980; 4th enlarged ed., Einsiedeln: Johannes Verlag, 1997. ET: *Mary, the Church at the Source.* San Francisco: Ignatius Press, 2005.

Das Fest des Glaubens: Versuche zur Theologie des Gottesdienstes. Einsiedeln: Johannes Verlag, 1981. ET: *The Feast of Faith: Approaches to a Theology of the Liturgy.* San Francisco: Ignatius Press, 1986.

Theologische Prinzipienlehre: Bausteine zur Fundamentaltheologie. Munich: Erich Wewel Verlag, 1982. ET: *Principles of Catholic Theology.* San Francisco: Ignatius Press, 1987.

"Transmission de la foi et sources de la foi". In Joseph Ratzinger et al. *Transmettre la foi aujourd'hui: Conférences données à Notre-Dame de Paris et à Notre-Dame de Fourvière.* Paris: Coopérative de l'Enseignement Religieux de Paris/Le Centurion, 1983. ET: "Handing on the Faith and the Sources of the Faith". In Joseph Ratzinger et al. *Handing on the Faith in an Age of Disbelief.* San Francisco: Ignatius Press, 2006, pp. 13–40.

Schauen auf den Durchbohrten: Versuche zu einer spirituellen Christologie. Einsiedeln: Johannes Verlag, 1984. ET: *Behold the Pierced One: An Approach to a Spiritual Christology.* San Francisco: Ignatius Press, 1986.

"Über die Hoffnung". In *Internationale katholische Zeitschrift Communio* 13 (1984): 293–305. ET: "On Hope". In *Communio* (American ed.) 12 (1985): 71–84.

Suchen was droben ist: Meditationen das Jahr hindurch. Freiburg im Breisgau: Herder, 1985. ET: *Seek That Which Is Above.* San Francisco: Ignatius Press, 1986.

Il cammino pasquale: Corso di esercizi spirituali tenuti in Vaticano alla presenza di S. S. Giovanni Paolo II. Milan: Ancora, 1985; 4th ed., 2006. ET: *Journey towards Easter: Retreat Given in the Vatican in the Presence of John Paul II.* Slough: St. Paul Publications, 1987. Also *Journey to Easter: Spiritual Reflections for the Lenten Season.* New York: Crossroad, 2006.

Rapporto sulla fede. With Vittorio Messori. Cinisello Balsamo: San Paolo, 1985. ET: *The Ratzinger Report: An Exclusive Interview on the State of the Church.* San Francisco: Ignatius Press, 1985.

Im Anfang schuf Gott: Vier Predigten über Schöpfung und Fall. Munich: Erich Wewel Verlag, 1986; 2nd enlarged ed. Einsiedeln: Johannes Verlag, 1996. ET: *In the Beginning: A Catholic Understanding of Creation and the Fall.* Grand Rapids: Eerdmans, 1995.

Kirche, Ökumene und Politik: Neue Versuche zur Ekklesiologie. Einsiedeln and Freiburg im Breisgau: Johannes Verlag, 1987. ET: *Church, Ecumenism and Politics: New Essays in Ecclesiology.* Slough: St. Paul Publications, 1988.

Diener eurer Freude: Meditationen über die priesterliche Spiritualität. Freiburg im Breisgau: Herder, 1988. ET: *Ministers of Your Joy: Meditations on Priestly Spirituality.* Slough: St. Paul Publications, 1989.

"Biblical Interpretation in Crisis: On the Question of the Foundations and Approaches of Exegesis Today". In *This World: A Journal of Religion and Public Life* 22 (Summer 1988): 1–19. Again in *Biblical Interpretation in Crisis: The Ratzinger Conference on Bible and Church.* Edited by R. J. Neuhaus. Grand Rapids: Eerdmans, 1989, pp. 1–23. Also in *The Essential Pope Benedict XVI: His Central Writings and Speeches.* Edited by John F. Thornton and Susan B. Varenne. San Francisco: HarperSanFrancisco, 2007, pp. 243–58.

Auf Christus schauen: Einübung in Glaube, Hoffnung, Liebe. Freiburg im Breisgau: Herder, 1989. ET: *The Yes of Jesus Christ: Exercises in Faith, Hope and Love.* New York: Crossroad, 2005. Originally published as *To Look on Christ: Exercises in Faith, Hope and Love.* New York: Crossroad, 1991.

Zur Gemeinschaft gerufen: Kirche heute verstehen. Freiburg: Herder, 1991. ET: *Called to Communion: Understanding the Church Today.* San Francisco: Ignatius Press, 1996.

Wendezeit für Europa? Diagnosen und Prognosen zur Lage von Kirche und Welt. Einsiedeln and Freiburg im Breisgau: Johannes Verlag, 1991. ET: *A Turning Point for Europe: The Church in the Modern World—Assessment and Forecast.* San Francisco: Ignatius Press, 1994.

"Wenn du Frieden willst, achte das Gewissen jedes Menschen: Gewissen und Wahrheit". In *Fides quaerens intellectum: Beiträge zur Fundamentaltheologie: M. Seckler zum 65. Geburtstag.* Edited by M. Kessler et al. Tübingen and Basel: Francke Verlag, 1992, pp. 293–309. An expanded version is published in *Wahrheit, Werte, Macht* (see below), pp. 27–62. ET: "Conscience and Truth". In *Crisis of Conscience.* Edited by John M. Haas. New York: Crossroad, 1996, pp. 1–20. Also in *Values in a Time of Upheaval* (see below), pp. 75–99.

Wesen und Aufgabe der Theologie. Einsiedeln and Freiburg im Breisgau: Johannes Verlag, 1993. ET: *The Nature and Mission of Theology: Approaches to Understanding Its Role in the Light of Present Controversy.* San Francisco: Ignatius Press, 1995.

Wahrheit, Werte, Macht: Prüfsteine der pluralistischen Gesellschaft. Freiburg im Breisgau: Herder, 1993. *Values in a Time of Upheaval* contains the English translation of the following essays: "Freedom, Law and the Good: Moral Principles in Democratic Societies"; "What is Truth? The Significance of Religious and Ethical Values in a Pluralistic Society"; "If You Want Peace ... Conscience and Truth".

Kleine Hinführung zum Katechismus der katholischen Kirche. With Christoph Schönborn. Munich: Neue Stadt, 1993. ET: *Introduction to the Catechism of the Catholic Church.* San Francisco: Ignatius Press, 1994.

Evangelium—Katechese—Katechismus: Streiflichter auf den Katechismus der katholischen Kirche. Munich: Neue Stadt, 1995. ET: *Gospel, Catechesis, Catechism: Sidelights on the Catechism of the Catholic Church.* San Francisco: Ignatius Press, 1997.

Ein neues Lied für den Herrn: Christusglaube und Liturgie in der Gegenwart. Freiburg im Breisgau: Herder, 1995. ET: *A New Song for the Lord: Faith in Christ and Liturgy.* New York: Crossroad, 1996.

Salz der Erde: Christentum und katholische Kirche an der Jahrtausendwende: Ein Gespräch mit Peter Seewald. Stuttgart: Deutsche Verlags-Anstalt, 1996. ET: *Salt of the Earth: Christianity and the Catholic Church at the End of the Millennium, An Interview with Peter Seewald.* San Francisco: Ignatius Press, 1997.

La via della fede: Le ragioni dell'etica nell'epoca presente. Milan: Ares, 1996. No English translation.

Bilder der Hoffnung: Wanderungen im Kirchenjahr. Freiburg im Breisgau: Herder, 1997. ET: *Images of Hope: Meditations on Major Feasts.* San Francisco: Ignatius Press, 2006.

La mia vita: Ricordi (1927–1977). Milan: San Paolo, 1997. ET: *Milestones: Memoirs 1927–1977.* San Francisco: Ignatius Press, 1998.

Vom Wiederauffinden der Mitte, Grundorientierung: Texte aus vier Jahrzehnten. Published by the Association of former students (*Schülerkreis*). Edited by S. O. Horn, V. Pfnür, V. Twomey, S. Wiedenhofer, and J. Zöhrer. Freiburg im Breisgau: Herder, 1997. No English translation.

Der Geist der Liturgie: Eine Einführung. Freiburg im Breisgau, Basel, and Vienna: Herder, 2000. ET: *The Spirit of the Liturgy.* San Francisco: Ignatius Press, 2000.

Gott und die Welt: Glauben und Leben in unserer Zeit: Ein Gespräch mit Peter Seewald. Stuttgart: Deutsche Verlags-Anstalt, 2000. ET:

God and the World: A Conversation with Peter Seewald. San Francisco: Ignatius Press, 2002.

Gott ist uns nah: Eucharistie: Mitte des Lebens. Edited by Stephan O. Horn and Vinzenz Pfnür. Augsburg: Sankt Ulrich Verlag, 2001. ET: *God Is Near Us: The Eucharist, the Heart of Life.* San Francisco: Ignatius Press, 2003.

Weggemeinschaft des Glaubens: Kirche als Communio. Augsburg: Sankt Ulrich Verlag, 2002. ET: *Pilgrim Fellowship of Faith: The Church as Communion.* San Francisco: Ignatius Press, 2005.

Glaube—Wahrheit—Toleranz: Das Christentum und die Weltreligionen. Freiburg im Breisgau: Herder, 2003. ET: *Truth and Tolerance: Christian Belief and World Religions.* San Francisco: Ignatius Press, 2004.

Unterwegs zu Jesus Christus. Augsburg: Sankt Ulrich Verlag, 2004. ET: *On the Way to Jesus Christ.* San Francisco: Ignatius Press, 2005.

Werte in Zeiten des Umbruchs: Die Herausforderungen der Zukunft bestehen. Freiburg im Breisgau: Herder, 2005. ET: *Values in a Time of Upheaval.* New York: Crossroad; San Francisco: Ignatius Press, 2006.

L'Europa di Benedetto nella crisi delle culture. Siena: Cantagalli, 2005. ET: *Christianity and the Crisis of Cultures.* San Francisco: Ignatius Press, 2006.

Gottes Glanz in unserer Zeit: Meditationen zum Kirchenjahr. Freiburg im Breisgau: Herder, 2005. Includes material earlier published in *Suchen was droben ist* and *Bilder der Hoffnung.*

Wer hilft uns leben? Von Gott und Mensch. Edited by Holger Zaborowski and Alwin Letzkus. Freiburg im Breisgau: Herder, 2005. No English translation.

Der Segen der Weihnacht Meditationen. Freiburg im Breisgau: Herder, 2005. ET: *The Blessing of Christmas.* San Francisco: Ignatius Press, 2007.

Komm Heiliger Geist! Pfingstpredigten, 2nd ed., Munich: Erich Wewel Verlag, 2005. No English translation.

Jesus von Nazareth: Von der Taufe im Jordan bis zur Verklärung. Freiburg: Herder, 2007. ET: *Jesus of Nazareth: From the Baptism in the Jordan to the Transfiguration.* New York: Doubleday, 2007.

MAGISTERIUM OF POPE BENEDICT XVI

Encyclical Letter *Deus Caritas Est,* December 25, 2005. Vatican City: Libreria Editrice Vaticana, 2006. ET: *God Is Love.* San Francisco: Ignatius Press, 2006.

God's Revolution: World Youth Day and Other Cologne Talks. San Francisco: Ignatius Press, 2006.

Encyclical Letter *Spe Salvi,* November 30, 2007. Vatican City: Libreria Editrice Vaticana, 2007. ET: *Saved in Hope.* San Francisco: Ignatius Press, 2008

HOMILIES AND ADDRESSES

The Holy Father's homilies and addresses at the 2005 World Youth Day celebrations in Cologne are contained in *God's Revolution* (see above). Other homilies or addresses mentioned in this book are listed below. Source references are to the weekly English-language edition of *L'Osservatore Romano* (abbreviated as OR).

All of Pope Benedict's addresses are available on the Vatican website at the following address: www.vatican.va/holy_father/benedict_xvi/index.htm.

Copyright for all Papal texts is held by the Libreria Editrice Vaticana.

Cardinal Joseph Ratzinger

Homily at the Mass for the election of the Roman Pontiff, April 18, 2005. In OR, April 20, 2005, p. 3.

Pope Benedict XVI

Homily at the Mass for the inauguration of the Pontificate, April 24, 2005. In OR, April 27, 2005, pp. 1, 8–9.

Address to the Clergy of the Diocese of Rome, May 13, 2005. In OR, May 18, 2005, pp. 3, 10.

Interview broadcast on Vatican Radio, August 15, 2005. Text available on the Vatican Radio website at the following link: www.oecumene.radiovaticana.org/en1/benedict_xvi_itv.asp.

Angelus, September 18, 2005. In OR, September 21, 2005, p. 1.

Homily at the Mass celebrated to mark the fortieth anniversary of the end of the Second Vatican Council, December 8, 2005. In OR, December 14, 2005, pp. 8–10.

Homily at the Mass for the Fourth Sunday of Advent, December 18, 2005. In OR, January 4, 2006, pp. 11, 14.

Address to the Roman Curia, December 22, 2005. In OR, January 4, 2006, pp. 4–6.

General Audience, February 15, 2006. In OR, February 22, 2006, p. 11.

Address to the Clergy of the Diocese of Rome, March 2, 2006. In OR, March 15, 2006, pp. 5–8.